THE CURRENCY OF TIME

A THREE BUCKET APPROACH TO

LIVE NOW AND RETIRE WHILE YOU WORK

DAVID W. ADAMS, CPA, CFP®

Advantage®

Published by Advantage, Charleston, South Carolina.
Member of Advantage Media Group.

ADVANTAGE is a registered trademark, and the Advantage colophon is a trademark of Advantage Media Group, Inc.

Printed in the United States of America.

10 9 8 7 6 5 4 3 2 1

ISBN: 978-1-64225-067-1
LCCN: 2018964060

Cover design by Melanie Cloth.
Layout design by Carly Blake.

To Wayne Adams, my selfless father, for teaching me the true value of spending time on experiences versus money on things. And to Martha Adams, my mother, who provided a loving, safe, and stable home.

The information contained in this book does not purport to be a complete description of the securities, markets, or developments referred to in this material. The information has been obtained from sources considered to be reliable, but we do not guarantee that the foregoing material is accurate or complete. Any information is not a complete summary or statement of all available data necessary for making an investment decision and does not constitute a recommendation. Any opinions of the chapter authors are those of the chapter author and not necessarily those of RJFS or Raymond James. Expressions of opinion are as of the initial book publishing date and are subject to change without notice. Raymond James Financial Services, Inc., is not responsible for the consequences of any particular transaction or investment decision based on the content of this book. All financial, retirement and estate planning should be individualized as each person's situation is unique.

This information is not intended as a solicitation or an offer to buy or sell any security referred to herein. Keep in mind that all investing involves risk and there is no assurance that our recommendations or strategies will ultimately be successful or profitable nor protect against a loss. There may also be the potential for missed growth opportunities that may occur after the sale of an investment. Recommendations, specific investments or strategies discussed may not be suitable for all investors. Past performance may not be indicative of future results. You should discuss any tax or legal matters with the appropriate professional.

Securities offered through Raymond James Financial Services, Inc., member FINRA/SIPC. Investment Advisory services offered through Raymond James Financial Services Advisors, Inc. David Adams Wealth Group is not a registered broker/dealer and is independent of Raymond James Financial Services, Inc. Raymond James is not affiliated with and does not endorse, authorize or sponsor any of the websites or entities contained in this material.

The examples given in this book are hypothetical in nature and are not intended to portray the actual outcome of any specific situation. Your individual situation is unique and your results will vary.

TABLE OF CONTENTS

INTRODUCTION

WHAT IT MEANS TO RETIRE WHILE YOU WORK

As I write this first sentence, I'm imagining that I'm helping many people.

That forty-five-year-old, stuck at his desk, thinking, *Will I ever start that magazine I've been dreaming of, or will I be stuck here forever, waiting on Social Security to kick in so I can finally quit?*

That college student who wants to get started on the right foot financially but doesn't know how.

That single mother who's working sixty hours a week, tending to two young daughters, and wondering, *Will I ever be able to spend more quality time with my kids and operate my own home business?*

That terrified sixty-three-year-old who's fatigued, working himself to near-death so he can reach some "magic number" to finally retire.

This last one hits close to home. As you'll learn, it was a big part of my "why" for this book.

Often, when people think about financial advisors, they think, *Oh, they can't help me. Financial advisors are for people who have a lot of money.*

Financial advisors can certainly help wealthy people optimize the returns on their investments and manage their tax burden. But that's not what this book is about. What gives me the most satisfaction is helping real people who are struggling to enjoy life through the daily challenges of raising families, toiling away at jobs they don't like, and worrying about the future.

As a financial planner and student of human behavior, I've spent years working with thousands of clients. Over that time I've noticed a trend that worries me: we're working ourselves into poor health, loneliness, and perpetual stress *just* to make it to retirement.

We do this because we want to generate enough money to sustain our lifestyles in our later years. We are letting the fear of not having enough, or being enough, to drive us into career-focused lives that drain us of joy and put us in the hospital—or worse. This has to change.

We must, together, find a way to maximize and enjoy our time—our most important, precious, and limited currency.

RETIREMENT SHOULDN'T MEAN WE STOP GROWING.

The problem with the word *retirement* is that it means to stop—to stop growing, contributing, and earning. If we aren't growing, we're dying. As humans, we're not wired to just *stop*. We need connection, love, mental stimulation, and purpose.

Stopping is counterintuitive to what the body needs. If you're meant to live until ninety, why stop living at sixty? The brain is a muscle, which means it has to be used to remain healthy. A 2016

Mayo Clinic study found that keeping mentally active and having intellectual pursuits in midlife might also delay the onset of symptoms of Alzheimer's.[1]

Instead of stopping completely, most people can maintain their health by working twenty or thirty hours a week, or working enough so they're able to pay basic expenses without having to worry about depleting their savings.

A 2016 Oregon State University study found that people who retired one year past age sixty-five had an 11 percent lower risk of death than those who retired at age sixty-five, even after accounting for demographic, lifestyle, and health issues.[2] Even people who described themselves as unhealthy had a 9 percent lower mortality risk working just one year past that age. Just imagine how working until age seventy-five or eighty could impact these stats.

Nowadays, pensions are as good as extinct. And they certainly don't work the way they used to. When I was an auditor with one of the "big four" public accounting firms, I consulted a major airline that gave pilots who had worked thirty years or more 80 percent or so of their salary for life. Although it's a noble gesture, this is unsustainable financially for most companies.

It's up to us to find a new model for balancing savings, work, health, and life—otherwise, we risk growing overwhelmed and hopeless, thinking we have to save rigorously to "retire" at sixty-five and sustain ourselves thereafter.

I'm here to tell you there's a much better way to live. Together, we'll unpack and rethink the old-school retirement methodology.

---

1 Maggie Fox. "Busy Brains Delay Alzheimer's Symptoms But Not the Disease." NBCNews.com, March 1, 2016, https://www.nbcnews.com/health/aging/busy-brains-delay-alzheimer-s-symptoms-not-disease-n529451.

2 Ann Brenoff, "Early Retirement May Be the Kiss of Death Study Finds," *Huffington Post*, April 28 2016, https://www.huffingtonpost.com/entry/early-retirement-may-be-the-kiss-of-death-study-finds_us_57221aa3e4b01a5ebde49eff.

COLLECT MEANINGFUL EXPERIENCES, NOT THINGS.

Money can't buy happiness, but it's easy to become a slave to things. Imagine you have a net worth of $30 million and homes all over the world. Now, imagine that you pay $60,000 per home for caretakers to maintain each of the properties—but you're not even sure whether or not they're doing a good job. Given a scenario like this, where your annual expenses can easily touch the millions, it's easy to see how you might worry that $30 million isn't enough—if only you had $40 million, you'd feel comfortable.

Not likely you say.

But I've witnessed stories *just like this* several times. Studies prove that when people become ultra-wealthy and accumulate stuff, they become slaves to that stuff and grow less connected to people. Research shows that the emotions and happiness you experience on a day-to-day basis slows down after your annual income hits about $75,000.[3]

I've read countless other studies that validate that happiness grows some as income gets to around the $150,000 per year mark, and then after that it begins to diminish. You might be thinking, *How could that be? You mean people who make $500,000 rather than $150,000 are less happy?*

Of course, this doesn't apply to everyone, but generally the answer is headed in the direction of yes. Once people reach a certain level of financial comfort or security, they simply use additional income to buy more stuff. And more stuff causes more problems.

3 Martha C. White, "This Is How Much Money You Should Be Making by the Time You're Forty," *Time*, July 26, 2017, http://time.com/money/4868997/how-much-money-make-age-40/.

One of my favorite musicians growing up, Eddie Vedder (oh yes, Pearl Jam), has a song called "Society" that has some amazing lines on this topic. Do a quick Google search for the lyrics, and you'll see what I mean. It reinforces my belief that when you accumulate more stuff, you need more space to store it all and that less is more.

It's a vicious cycle of money and greed—unless we find a way to enjoy our lives and relationships, outside the money. The money simply becomes a means to an end, allowing us to pay for the experiences and memories we share with people we love, not just buy more stuff.

The more stuff people have, the more time, money, and effort they spend keeping track of it. If you have six cars, you have to get oil changes, buy new tires, and keep the batteries charged in all six of them. If you own four homes, you have to pay for caretakers, replace appliances, keep up with taxes, and maintain the lawn for all four of them. It goes on and on.

Instead of accumulating things or striving to keep *X* amount of dollars in your accounts, why not strive for more balance in your life by focusing on creating meaningful experiences with the people you love? This will lead to happy days, shared memories, and, one hopes, an incredible legacy. The depth of your relationships are measured by the number of *Remember when* ... moments you have with loved ones, not your bank account.

I've spoken to a handful of clients in their final days, and not once did anyone talk about money. Any words of wisdom they left for me or their kids had to do with the joy they had in their hearts from sharing meaningful experiences with loved ones. Also, when I asked them what regrets they had, every single time it was the same: wishing they had shared more of these experiences with family and friends. No talk of money, period. You can't take it with you. And anyway, who cares to be remembered as the richest man in the graveyard?

As one of my favorite clients always says, "David, my goal is to die bouncing my last check, living life to its fullest."

A BROKEN INDUSTRY

The financial services industry trains financial advisors to calculate how much money you need to retire and then encourages you to live off that money and spend it down. For most people, the numbers aren't just way out of reach, they're also demotivating. This is where the fear originates. People think they'll never have enough to retire comfortably, so they keep working, ignoring other important aspects of their lives.

The industry trains advisors to focus only on how much clients are saving and how much they will have at the "end" of the journey. Most people define this end as the time when they stop working, either because they want to retire or because they are physically no longer able to work.

Our industry focuses obsessively on the numbers rather than the feelings and experiences that make up a healthy retirement mind-set. Yes, I said it. The industry is broken. It needs an overhaul and new thought leadership. I'm convinced that this newer, more holistic way of viewing money, retirement, and life balance must be shared, and I'm committed to doing just that. This industry has rewarded me in so many ways—mainly in being able to make a huge difference in my clients' lives—and I want to give back and share my heart, even if it means bucking the traditional system.

Many people complain that advisors in this industry are coached to focus solely on encouraging clients to keep saving more money because, after all, investment advisors get paid on what they manage.

So, of course, they want you to save more because they get paid more, right? In my opinion, this is a conflict of interest. If a financial advisor tells a client to take a bunch of money out of an investment or retirement account to buy a dream house or a boat or to travel the world, it means he or she will make less money. When I first got into this business, I knew I did not want to run my practice that way.

Instead, I wanted to get to know each client, be a good listener, and give the best advice I could to help make them a happier, more well-rounded person. I believe in the abundance mentality more than the scarcity mentality—there's plenty of money and amazing clients to go around.

I am challenging my own industry's outdated view on retirement, and I can't wait to offer my perspective on this topic to anyone who will listen. I wrote this book in the hopes of liberating you from the self-defeating belief that you have to work yourself into the ground, worry about money your entire life, and enter retirement full of fear about the future.

I am here to help you find ways to savor the only currency that truly matters: *time.*

Retirement is a journey, not a destination. There is a much better way!

A BETTER WAY: RETIRE WHILE YOU WORK

Once you realize and understand that time is the real currency in life, your mind-set starts to change. By retiring while you work, you can find ways to enjoy every day of your life, regardless of which stage you're currently in.

What if you could do what you're passionate about and achieve work-life balance? What if you were relieved of the pressure to have some massive amount saved? My approach is to create fluid life financial plans, not emergency retirement plans.

I believe we can find joy in the journey of life while still satisfying our ambitions, goals, health, and personal and spiritual lives. If we learn to prioritize living life while also planning for the future, we can find the kind of work-life balance that fuels dreams. I've seen this up close with many of my dearest clients. I admire them. I strive to follow in their footsteps. And I commit to sharing their recipes for success with other clients who are stuck.

And please know this—you do *not* have to have millions of dollars, a six-figure income, or a life with no responsibilities to find your way toward retiring while you work. Often, we read books like this and immediately think, *Must be nice, but I could never do those things because* (insert a million different real-life roadblocks here). And I get it. There are financial obstacles you may face while reading this book. But what if I told you that you can get out of debt and build your three buckets (which I'll explain in detail throughout this book), even with limited resources? It just takes some creativity.

For example, say you and your significant other are in your early thirties, and you're both working sixty hours a week, earning a salary of $50,000 per year. Your spouse decides to take time off from their job as a nurse and is considering a master's program to increase their salary long term. You both need a break, and want to explore the world before your spouse starts school and you consider starting a family. But how? The idea of saving up hundreds of thousands of dollars before you can do this is overwhelming, frustrating, and perhaps outright depressing. You're thinking, *David, how the heck do we retire while we work, or even get a taste of that by stepping out of the rat race long enough so we don't burn ourselves out?* Great question. Let's look at your hypothetical finances and I'll explain how I would answer this question if you were a client.[4]

Let's say you have $8,000 in an emergency fund savings and $11,000 in a retirement account and owe $180,000 on your home, which is worth $250,000. The idea of travelling the world for six months and liquidating all of your savings and retirement assets plus accumulating more debt seems foolish, right? Let's think outside the box, and come up with a solution:

- The housing rental market, both short-term and long-term, is pretty hot in your town (say Nashville, for instance). Let's say we listed your home for rent, fully furnished, and found a tenant willing to sign a six-month contract for $2,000 per month. Say your mortgage, lawn care, and other miscellaneous home costs are $1,500 per month. This gives you a positive cash flow of $500 per month.

- You've read travel blogs on people who lived on $30 a day all over the world, and wanted to try this approach, living modestly but experiencing abundantly. Your cost would be around $6,000 for 6 months.

- You quit your job and take six months to work on your business plan, start a podcast, and look for other sources of income until you can make money doing what you love.

- Over these six months, you'll have $3,000 of excess cash from your home being rented ($500/month x 6 months),

4 As a financial planner, in a highly regulated industry, we are not allowed to have client testimonials or use actual client examples—only hypotheticals. I pitched a fit like a toddler to our compliance department, then pouted, and moved on. Throughout this book, I will illustrate examples and situations I have seen over my career. After all, this book is about you and me helping you on your journey, not about me.

meaning your net cost of travelling the world for 6 months would be only $3,000 ($6,000 for $30/day travel for 6 months, minus the $3,000 excess from home)!

- When you return, you'll still have your savings and retirement intact and feel ready to start the next chapter of your life.

It's one thing to talk about these retire-while-you-work concepts and another to witness them in action, changing lives. While they may not be possible for everyone, I think you'd be surprised at what you can accomplish if you get creative enough.

That's why *I love this job*—because retiring while you work is possible at every level of wealth. There's always a way to achieve it on some scale, for almost anyone. It's a mind-set that requires a focus on balancing your family, work, financial planning, and physical and spiritual health. It's a concept that takes time to understand and implement using my *three buckets* approach. But once you do it, you'll feel free, joyful, and fulfilled. You will start to maximize the currency of time. No cheesy gimmicks here—this stuff works, and it changes lives. I've seen it hundreds of times, and it's reversed the way I think about money from the antiquated methods our industry trains us in.

Here are the three parts I've divided this book into:

- **PART 1** explains the "why, what, and how" of my retire-while-you-work philosophy. Once you understand why this is all so important, we can build from that foundation.

- **PART 2** shares real-life solutions to common questions and situations I've witnessed in meetings with thousands of people over the past fifteen years. The answers I provide aren't fluff or hard-to-understand industry jargon. They're real-life, kitchen table-talk answers—the same ones I'd give you if we sat face-to-face.

- **PART 3** shares some valuable lessons that tie everything together and holistically put you on the path toward retiring while you work and managing your time.

I'll end this introduction by saying this: I'm an open book (pun intended), and I welcome any questions I may have not addressed in this first edition of my book. Email me anytime at david.w.adams@raymondjames.com, or visit davidadamswealthgroup.com or retirewhileyouwork.com. I love meeting new people and sharing my passion.

I hope you get as much out of these pages as I have sharing the advice in them.

PART 1

RETIRE WHILE YOU WORK—AN EFFECTIVE STRATEGY

CHAPTER 1

LESSONS FROM MY FATHER

When my dad was a child, he was abandoned by his father. At the age of fourteen, he lost his mother, and then at seventeen, his grandmother. Although he had a court-appointed guardian, he was living alone by sixteen with the parents of his neighborhood friends keeping watch after him.

I cannot imagine how he must've felt—losing both his mother and grandmother and knowing his father was out there somewhere, yet he was all alone. He could easily have chosen to not have a family, show love, or make sacrifices for others. For many, what he'd suffered would have been reason enough to build an impenetrable barrier around their hearts. But instead, my dad used the hurt as motivation to be the best father and husband possible, and to love big.

My parents provided a stable home and childhood for both my sister and me. While we were growing up, they were frugal, paid for things in cash, and lived well beneath their means. We didn't have anything flashy, but we didn't want for anything, either—we were considered middle class. Sure, I often wished I had the cool new Michael Jordan Nike shoes when they came out, or the cool-kid designer jeans. But I had all I needed, was loved, and felt safe.

My dad is my hero—no question. He was, and still is, one of the most selfless people I know. For a man who grew up basically unloved and without any stability of his own, all he ever wanted was to be with his family and make us happy. I often wonder, how could a man deprived of love learn to love so well? He gave up countless opportunities to travel and make more money, choosing us even when we (mostly I) thought only of what we wanted.

Despite working long hours in a physically demanding job, my dad was a coach and line judge for some of my sports teams. He attended all my games—and there were lots of them, because I played four different sports. I remember him teaching me how to dribble a basketball with both hands. I was a point guard, and every time I crossed the half-court line, I would dribble to the right, and the other team would steal the ball. But not for long. One day, I got to that line, did a little spin move, and dribbled with my left hand—game over. I'll never forget Dad practicing with me in the driveway after a long day's work to perfect that NBA-worthy move.

Twice a year, we took a road trip to Florida. Those long car rides in the good old Dodge Caravan (you know, the one with the wood grain down the side) were unforgettable. My sister and I each had our own row to sprawl out in, eat candy, and read whatever it is we read at that age while the Beatles, Crosby Stills & Nash, and James Taylor played on repeat.

CHASING THE "MAGIC NUMBER"

My father was a hard-working retail manager for forty years. He made a decent living working himself silly and, close to retirement, had saved up a respectable nest egg. But when he hit his early sixties, his body started giving out. Retail had kept him in stockrooms doing manual labor for four decades.

He'd worked himself too hard for years in pursuit of his "magic age"—sixty-seven—when he thought he'd hit the "magic number." The magic age is the age you think you should retire, while the magic number is the amount of money you think you need to retire comfortably.

My dad's goal was self-induced, rooted little in fact or reality, and was based on what the financial planning industry and the Average Joe was doing. By sixty-three, he didn't think he had enough and was afraid to retire before his Social Security kicked in.

The magic age and magic number are myths. They're also the plot of countless brokerage-firm commercials, encouraging you to chase the arrows to that imaginary number. Conventional wisdom would have us believe that $1 million or a retirement income of 80 percent of your current salary is a good safety net.

This may sound good, but it's a pretty big generalization. Most people wouldn't be able to save that kind of a money in a couple of lifetimes. Most people would hear these numbers, get overwhelmed, and give up, thinking they'll never retire.

But not anymore. I have a solution that can help make this broken process easier than you could have hoped.

HEALTH ISSUES, RETIREMENT'S WORST ENEMY

My mom and I noticed that Dad was working too much and not enjoying life enough. It upset us to watch this, and we'd tell him to slow down. He'd listen for a minute, but would end up resuming his habit—it was just ingrained in him. He had an old-fashioned work ethic, and I respected the heck out of that, but only to a point.

He was so selfless, that instead of having his assistant managers check on a fire alarm or unload inventory at four o'clock in the morning, he'd often do it himself, wanting them to sleep longer or spend extra time with their families. While that was thoughtful, the downside was that he worked himself harder than he needed to in his early sixties. His mind was telling him he needed to work 'til sixty-seven and save *X* amount of money, but his body was telling a different story.

One day, when my dad was sixty-three, I was sitting in a staff meeting when my sister, who's a nurse, kept calling, which was unusual. Usually, we text (yes, so personal our society has become). When I answered my phone, she said, "Did you hear about Dad?"

My heart stopped. She told me he'd been rushed to the emergency room. I burst into tears in the middle of the meeting, rushed to my car, and drove from Nashville to Memphis. The doctors thought he'd suffered a stroke. As it turned out, his blood pressure had shot through the roof—and he hadn't had a stroke, thank God. But it was a horrific scare nonetheless.

At hearing the news, a rush of emotions overcame me—elation that he was going to be okay, frustration that he wouldn't stop working, sadness that he was going through this, and anger toward his company for working him so hard. I told him, "Dad, you've got to quit. You're retiring today. You're done."

He said, "David, I just need some more sleep. I have to work a bit longer. You're sweet for worrying about me, but I'm fine."

"Dad, there's no way I'm losing you to retail," I said, dead serious. "It's just not going to happen. You've got to quit. You're done." We were at an emotional stalemate.

After several days of discussion, sharing hugs, tears, and emotions, I finally convinced him to quit. As I helped write his resignation letter, I was so proud of him, because I thought it would take years for him to take that step. When he actually turned it in that Monday, I was shocked.

He told me, "When I was on that stretcher, all I could think about was leaving your mom a widow. I thought I was dying, and I just wanted another chance so badly. I'll never forget that feeling."

But then he admitted that he was scared about money. He said, "I'm not going to forget that moment. It's not about the money, but I'm a little scared about the money. Can you help me look at our finances?"

"Yes, of course," I said, relishing the opportunity to connect and grow closer with him.

So we did. Through the process, we bonded and shared some deep feelings, fears, and experiences, and my dad even opened up about his childhood experiences. It was a sweet, precious period, and I'm so blessed to have had that opportunity with my father after his near-death experience.

I do want to take a moment to add that my mother is, and always has been, the family's foundation. Without her love and selfless support, the rest of us would be a complete mess. I love you, Mom.

During that period, I had to grow up fast—as both a son and financial planner. The student in me had to take on the role of teacher. My dad needed me—he had groomed me for this since I was a little boy. It felt good to be able to step up to the plate and help out.

After he turned in his resignation, my mom and I threw him a surprise retirement party. On his last day at work, customers he had known for years lined up with presents, hugging him and wishing him well. Apparently, putting others first and having a heart the size of Tennessee leaves an impact on people and will amass you a deep level of authentic respect. Common sense for many, maybe, but a lesson learned for a self-focused, early-thirties professional (yours truly).

My dad's story is why I'm so passionate about the subject of retiring while you work, which has shaped who I'm becoming as a financial advisor. I want to help redefine what retirement looks like. We need to stop making it so that retirement means hospital stays, medical bills, and the inability to enjoy a life of leisure.

> **We need to stop making it so that retirement means hospital stays, medical bills, and the inability to enjoy a life of leisure.**

Walking side by side with my father during that emotional transition into retirement changed my entire perspective on what I do and how I advise clients every day. Sure, I'd helped thousands of people through similar transitions and scares, but there's something about experiencing it firsthand alongside an immediate family member that makes the ordeal take on a greater impact. Now I want to share this journey with others and help them apply the best practices for their lives.

LEARNING THE VALUE OF A DOLLAR

When I was growing up, I remember wanting to be financially responsible and secure, just like my parents. It started at age nine with baseball cards. I'd set up a table in the driveway, lining up the cards that featured all my top players and my *Beckett* magazine to value each of them. My buddies and I would buy, sell, and trade cards with our allowances. Soon this empire grew to include football and basketball cards. And then when I turned thirteen, it was time to go big or go home. So I decided to start a lawn-mowing business.

My dad offered me his old, beat-up Briggs & Stratton mower for $25. I thought it was so mean for him to make me buy it—I mean, who makes their kid do that? My partner and childhood best friend, Jason, had a new mower each summer, paid for by his father. Little did I know that this lesson would later frame the way I viewed and valued a dollar.

You see, because I had skin in the game, every single evening after mowing the neighbors' yards, I'd clean that mower and get it ready for the next day. Each spring, I'd change the oil and spark plugs, sharpen the blade, and tighten the wheels, because I had to get as many miles on Old Faithful as I could. Would I have taken as much care of it had my dad just given it to me? At that age, definitely not.

I loved saving and the feeling of building long-term financial security. Today, nearly thirty years later, I get to help my clients manage their hard-earned dollars.

LEARNING THE VALUE OF TIME AND EXPERIENCES WITH LOVED ONES

While being financially responsible is important, the next lesson my father would teach me was even more important: no amount of money can substitute for the value of time and experiences in life with loved ones. Money and things will never provide true happiness or fulfillment.

No amount of money can substitute for the value of time and experiences in life with loved ones.

When I was in college and totally self-absorbed, my dad told me that the way you spelled *love* was *time*. His words didn't resonate much with me then, but later, in my twenties, I started to listen and appreciate his wisdom more. I was mostly focused on building my financial planning practice, but these words slowly started to impact me. This lesson from my father is what reshaped my thinking of the word "currency," and how it really wasn't money, but instead, time.

And then, in my early thirties, after I had built a very successful practice, I experienced some major transitions and pain. I left my firm to start my own practice (think Jerry McGuire), fought a two-year legal battle, and got divorced in the same year after a brief marriage. It was during this, my deepest period of hurt and self-reflection, that I almost lost my father in his near-death experience.

That experience is what drove home his point for me: the true value of life is the time and experiences we share with loved ones. Money and jobs come and go, but love and memories endure.

THRIVING IN RETIREMENT

Four years later, Dad's sixty-seven, and he's doing great. His health is a lot better, and he has reconnected, even more deeply than before, with Mom. They go on walks every day and recently celebrated forty-three years of marriage.

Dad said it took about three months just to unwind. He hadn't slept more than four hours a night for twenty years, and after that, he started sleeping six or seven hours a night. His blood pressure went down, and he even looked healthier.

He did some volunteering, and he got a job working fifteen hours a week to help him cover his health insurance costs. He did that for about a year, but now he's fully retired and enjoys spending time with his grandchildren—and of course, his son (and financial advisor).

I'm beyond proud of my father for his recent retirement, and my heart is full as I watch my parents reconnect, shed stress, and start to find themselves again. This entire experience has made it clear that my calling is to help others solve the misconception of retirement.

This is my "why."

CHAPTER 2

WE NEED A DIFFERENT RETIREMENT MODEL TO FOLLOW

A few years ago, I began questioning my priorities. In my early thirties, I was fortunate enough to reach what most would consider the pinnacle of success. I had a big house in a desirable area of town, was financially set, had reached a tremendous level of success within my business, and was well-respected within my industry. But even with all that, something was missing. Despite my achievements and status, I didn't feel whole.

So I spent the next five years investing time and money in self-discovery and personal development. I found a mentor, participated in several retreats, and spoke to people whom I felt could help me reframe my view on life. I would leave each experience feeling such excitement about the wisdom and knowledge I was gaining. I knew that, through this self-work, I could make a positive impact on the lives of my clients, family members, and friends. My energy and determination quadrupled, and I'm eternally grateful for the lessons I've learned.

Those friends and mentors helped crystallize something for me: I learned that chasing financial security and success is only half the story. I was allowing the money I had in the bank, my pursuit of clients, and my professional success to systematically take over my life. I was so focused on the idea of being successful that I had become overworked, overstressed, and repressed. The truth is, I had completely lost sight of what matters the most: relationships, family, self-care, and the simple act of enjoying life.

MY PERSONAL JOURNEY THROUGH SELF-DEVELOPMENT

Thanks to the guidance I received, I stepped back and examined my priorities. What you spend time on is where your priorities lie. I was spending a lot of time in client meetings and at work-related events. There was a huge imbalance between the time I spent at work and the time I spent with my family and friends, doing things I enjoyed outside of work.

So I helped launch and host a men's group at my home, making an effort to connect with close friends, coworkers, and family members on a regular basis. Before that, I'd been spreading myself so thin that I wasn't making true connections with anyone (other than people at work for business). I decided to focus on placing my spiritual needs at the top of my priority list. For the previous decade, that top spot had been reserved for building my identity around my career. I quit trying to be the "lord of my own ring" and followed the sign that sits above my desk at my office. It's a verse from Psalm 46:10: "Be still, and know that I am God."

Giving up control was and is the hardest part of the process, especially because I'm a type A personality. But once I realized that we simply aren't in control, everything became easier, clearer, and more fulfilling. Unfortunately, it took me getting knocked down and stepped on to realize this.

I decided that the money and the security it brought is important, but by no means is it worth obsessing over at the expense of relationships, health, and happiness. This piece of wisdom can change your life. It changed mine and continues to do so.

RETIREMENT SHOULD BE FILLED WITH JOY, NOT FEAR.

I have seen hundreds of people in their sixties who are tired and scared. They're still working, but they feel like they haven't reached that magic number yet, so they think they don't have enough money to retire. Even clients with millions of dollars feel like they can't retire. That's how warped our society is when it comes to retirement. We have these arbitrary numbers in our minds that are typically fear-based. Or possibly even worse, greed-based.

And then, when they finally do retire, these clients are sometimes in such poor health that they can't enjoy their retirement. They have no identity outside their jobs, they're bored to death, and they don't have any hobbies. Often, they grow depressed—I've witnessed this scenario many times. From my experience, after people retire, it takes about two to three months for them to settle into their new lifestyle. At first, it's kind of exciting to be able to leisurely do even the small, day-to-day things, like running errands in the middle of the day or having the time to keep the house clean. But the excitement usually wears off fairly soon.

Many retirees realize their personal lives, without work, are empty. Maybe they had a shallow marriage or didn't really connect with the kids. So they try to connect, but sometimes by then it's too late. They can't identify their true purpose, and they feel a void deep in their gut.

Too often, when people grow bored after retirement, they rush back to work. And sometimes, they end up right back where they were—in a stressful work environment.

It's important to have retirement goals and a financial plan. But that's only part of the puzzle. If hard-working people like my dad obsess over the all-consuming magic number, they'll spend their lives working themselves ragged and never actually living.

According to a 2017 Gallup survey, 54 percent of US adults are worried about not having enough money for retirement and not being able to pay for medical costs resulting from a serious illness or accident. These two concerns have typically been the most worrisome for Americans since Gallup began conducting surveys in 2001 on people's eight most common financial worries. Luckily, that number is lower than what it was in 2016 when 64 percent were worried about retirement funds and 60 percent were concerned about affording medical costs. Although the percentage has declined, the fact remains that, even today, there's still confusion and fear.[5]

A movement needs to happen to break this mentality. Every time a client leaves my office with a big sigh of relief, leaving that worry at the door and giving me a big hug, every fiber in my being is activated, and I'm reminded why I love this job—my calling.

5 "Americans' Financial Worries Ease in 2017," Gallup News, http://news.gallup.com/poll/210890/americans-financial-anxieties-ease-2017.aspx.

CORPORATE AMERICA: VALUING WORK OVER WELL-BEING

Once I made changes in my own life, I started noticing the same workaholic tendencies in many of my clients. Their careers were taking an unhealthy hold of them. They were spending decades working themselves to the bone to achieve some unattainable goal of success and financial stability.

That's the story most of us share today. Corporate America has taught us not only to work hard but also to overwork ourselves. We're awarded a badge of honor for working weekends, and we're promoted for outshining coworkers by pulling sixty-hour work weeks.

As a CPA, I worked in the public accounting industry for a while, where your worth is defined by hours worked. My boss, a partner at the firm, was in his early forties and had three young boys. He worked from six in the morning until eight in the evening every day "to beat traffic."

One day, I asked him, "When do you get to see your kids?"

His answer horrified me: "On the weekends."

He was serious—yuck.

We're taught that success comes from climbing the ladder. More money, more stability, and more success are always just beyond the horizon.

Sadly, we invest the best years of our lives trading vacations, friends, and hobbies for work, only to feel empty and dissatisfied at the end. We have forgotten to enjoy the journey.

Sadly, we invest the best years of our lives trading vacations, friends, and hobbies for work, only to feel empty and dissatisfied at the end. We have forgotten to enjoy the journey.

But I'm here to remind you to enjoy it.

VACATIONS KEEP US HEALTHY AND REFRESHED.

Did you know that only 23 percent of employees use all their eligible time off? The average employee uses only about 54 percent of their vacation time—a number that hasn't changed much over the years. And when people do take vacation days, they aren't vacationing the entire time. Two-thirds (66 percent) report working on vacation, which is higher than in 2014 (61 percent).[6]

We need to take vacations and leave work behind. Vacations are fun, but they can also save your life. One study of men at high risk for coronary artery disease found that those who failed to take annual vacations were 32 percent more likely to die of a heart attack. And in the long-running Framingham Heart Study, women who vacationed just once every six years were eight times more likely to develop coronary artery disease or have a heart attack than women who vacationed twice a year.[7]

Some people don't take vacations because they feel guilty leaving coworkers to carry the burden of their work. Others fear that work they delegate won't get done right. And many others hoard vacation time because they're afraid of getting laid off or fired and want to be able to cash out the paid time when they leave their jobs.

By failing to take paid time off, we're robbing ourselves of happiness and saving money in fear that we won't have enough. I knew this from my own experiences and those of clients', but it was my dad's story that really brought me to my knees.

---

6 Kate Ashford, "Why American's Aren't Taking Half of Their Vacation Days," *Forbes*, May 31, 2017, https://www.forbes.com/sites/kateashford/2017/05/31/vacation/#e540ff9726a1.

7 "50 Ways to Live a Longer, Healthier Life," *AARP Bulletin*, March 2017, https://www.aarp.org/health/healthy-living/info-2017/50-ways-to-live-longer.html.

A MISSED OPPORTUNITY IN CORPORATE AMERICA

When my dad retired, his mind was still sharp, and he wanted an opportunity to continue contributing his forty years of experience to his company. But they weren't interested.

It was a put-off to see his company—and corporate America in general—operate this way. His company wouldn't give him a part-time job with a moderate salary and full health benefits (which he really needed). They denied him the joy of continuing to contribute, and they denied themselves forty years of valuable experience and wisdom, which Dad would have been happy to share with other employees. I couldn't understand why they wouldn't allow him to stay engaged and keep his health insurance until Medicare kicked in. But, because he was physically worn down, they couldn't think outside the corporate box to find a win-win and take advantage of his razor-sharp mind.

My type A personality compelled me to draft an email to the CEO and search for flights to the headquarters for an uninvited face-to-face "meeting." That never happened because my dad is a little more reserved than I am. Basically, he told me that if I confronted the CEO, I was grounded.

The way corporations ignore older workers is upsetting. A December 2017 article from CNBC revealed that dozens of companies use Facebook to exclude older workers from job ads.[8] For example, Verizon placed an ad on Facebook to recruit applicants for a unit focused on financial planning and analysis. The article says, "The ad showed a smiling, Millennial-aged woman seated at a computer and

8 Julia Angwin, ProPublica; Noam Scheiber, *The New York Times*; and Ariana Tobin, ProPublica, "Dozens of Companies Are Using Facebook to Exclude Older Workers from Job Ads," CNBC, December 20, 1017, https://www.cnbc.com/2017/12/20/companies-use-facebook-to-exclude-older-workers-from-job-ads.html.

promised that new hires could look forward to a rewarding career in which they would be 'more than just a number.' The promotion was set to run on the Facebook feeds of users 25 to 36 years old who lived in the nation's capital, or had recently visited there, and had demonstrated an interest in finance. For a vast majority of the hundreds of millions of people who check Facebook every day, the ad did not exist."

This is a *huge* problem in corporate America today. Companies are missing the boat! If you have a pool of sixty-somethings who are smart, experienced, and likely will live until age eighty or ninety and still need income but just aren't as physically fast anymore, why not let them retire while they work instead of letting them go? There's huge opportunity here.

In an article in the *University of Chicago Law Review*, Michael Stein, visiting professor at Harvard Law School, and his coauthors argue that retaining older workers is in everyone's best interest. They say that the financial costs of Social Security and Medicare are unsustainable and that pensions are dwindling as baby boomers live longer.[9] So accommodating older workers is to the economic benefit of the country—and to the social benefit of those who want to continue to work.

Many of these people aren't even ready to retire; they want to stay engaged, interact with people, and connect. They're aware of the benefits of continuing work in a limited capacity, but few companies give them that opportunity. This needs to change—now.

---

9 Ally Day, "Our Aging Population Needs Adjustments; We Have to Find a Way to Provide Them," *Slate*, December 27, 2017, http://www.slate.com/blogs/better_life_lab/2017/12/27/our_aging_population_means_changing_the_way_workplaces_deal_with_disability.html.

THE AARP IS GETTING IT RIGHT.

The American Association of Retired Persons (AARP) is an advocate for people over the age of fifty and has started something called the Employer Pledge Program.

This program is a national effort to help employers solve current and future staffing challenges and to direct older job seekers to employers that value and hire experienced workers. Working with AARP, participating organizations have signed a pledge stating that they do the following:

- believe in equal opportunity for all workers, regardless of age,
- believe that workers who are fifty and older should have a level playing field in their ability to compete for and obtain jobs,
- recognize the value of experienced workers, and
- recruit across diverse age groups and consider all applicants on an equal basis.[10]

As AARP demonstrates, we need a new model for our aging population and a new concept for retirement—retiring while you work.

10 "Employer Pledge Program," AARP, accessed October 2018, https://www.aarp.org/work/job-search/employer-pledge-companies/.

CHAPTER 3

LIVE TODAY WHILE WORKING FOR TOMORROW

Retiring while you work is a way of life that lets you live today while planning for tomorrow. It's not about finding a magic number, working yourself into bad health, or worrying your whole life about what will happen at the end of it. It's about finding ways to balance your passions, your work, and your home life.

We don't want to wake up at sixty-five and realize we've missed out on all of life's important things, such as spending time with family and friends and having unique life experiences. Retiring while you work is a philosophy that lets you work and sustain yourself while you keep engaged in life through things like exercise, love, stress management, financial freedom, connections, and spiritual health. I believe you must find balance in these aspects of life before you can truly achieve the retire-while-you-work mind-set.

When you don't find this balance, it's like walking through life blindfolded—working hard to reach some arbitrary goal of "enough money" or "the American dream" (the cliché of clichés). Too many people replace the anxiety of retiring comfortably with fear of the stock market, political agendas, or myriad other things completely out of their control.

But starting today, whether you're still in college, mid-career, or are looking to slow down soon, you and I can lead the movement to redefine how we work, live, and retire. It's time to understand, and put in place, a plan that helps you balance and enjoy life while responsibly saving for the future.

So where do you start? By adjusting your views about life and work.

WHAT RETIRING WHILE YOU WORK LOOKS LIKE

Retiring while you work means living a balanced life during your prime working years. It means blending your passions, work, and family time, regardless of your age or life stage.

If money weren't a consideration, what would you do with your life? How would you spend your time? Whatever your answer, those are the things you need to make time for right now.

Do you want to inspire your family to give back? Maybe your family would like to take a mission trip. If volunteering is important to you in your thirties, why not challenge yourself to volunteer two hours per quarter? And then, in your forties, three hours per quarter? Once you reach your fifties, maybe you'll start your own business and take two weeks at a time to volunteer.

It's all about setting goals to live a more holistic life. It's about filling your life with more than just working and saving. At our firm, we've implemented a new activity. One day per quarter, we volunteer throughout the community. Never once has there been a single ounce of regret for those hours spent. Better yet, every single time we walk away talking about how we feel re-energized, grateful, and more connected than before.

We have clients who've worked for decades, but who then spent the last few years of their corporate lives doing something they're passionate about, like becoming a personal trainer or teaching yoga while still working their regular jobs. It's like a second act, making the transition from work to retirement much smoother. Often, these passion careers end up fulfilling and energizing them mentally, emotionally, and financially for decades after they retire from their long-term careers.

Retiring while you work means living a balanced life during your prime working years. It means blending your passions, work, and family time, regardless of your age or life stage.

In all of these scenarios, people were able to buy themselves more time to invest in activities that mattered to them. Please don't read this book thinking it's only doable for people who have unlimited resources, the world's most flexible job, or the coolest boss. Even if you're making $30,000 a year, you can bring more balance to your life by simply challenging yourself and starting in small doses.

Retirement is a process that starts in your thirties and continues through your eighties and beyond. In your thirties, you're working hard and gaining momentum in your career, but to balance out your life, maybe you'll challenge yourself to take two family vacations a year.

In your forties, maybe you'll take a two-week cruise, spend more time visiting family, pick up an extra hobby, or play more golf. And then in your fifties and sixties, instead of obsessing over retirement, you'll pursue a passion, like opening a restaurant or clothing boutique, renovating houses, or doing some consulting. Whatever you choose should be a project devoid of stress that you enjoy and can do into your sixties, seventies, and beyond. It should be an art—not a tedious, boring job that keeps you chained to a desk. Oftentimes, by making this transition, people are able to work longer.

Because not only are they having fun, they're generating income, too. Even if you're making half of what you made in your full-time job, you won't have to obsess about stopping work or amassing an ungodly amount of debt. This approach makes those magic numbers your financial planner showed you meaningless, giving you a chance to create your own retirement plan and calculate realistic goals as you continue earning from a job you enjoy.

Using a systematic approach to transition gradually toward retirement also takes pressure off and allows you to relish time and experiences with family and friends while you work toward your retirement goals.

Using a systematic approach to transition gradually toward retirement also takes pressure off and allows you to relish time and experiences with family and friends while you work toward your retirement goals, like my father taught me to do. Again, this industry trains us to use spreadsheets and projections and to tell you how much money you will have at age sixty-five and how much you will need to last you until you die. So we come up with this big number, because it assumes you will never make another dollar in your life. Wrong.

It's really intimidating, and it scares people. A lot of times, it gives them "paralysis by analysis." They get overwhelmed and don't do anything. I quickly realized this was a flawed approach. "Retiring while you work" is a much better approach and has helped hundreds of our clients.

FIVE BASIC CONCEPTS OF RETIRING WHILE YOU WORK

After years of working with experts, coupled with my own experiences and those of my clients', I've discovered five basic concepts that support the retire-while-you-work plan.

Practicing these five concepts will get you in the right mind-set to find the work-life balance you crave. Take your time, find what works for you, and start living your life today. Let's take a look.

1. YOU DON'T NEED TO LOVE YOUR JOB TO LOVE YOUR LIFE.

There's a dangerous mind-set today that we're not doing life right if we're not doing meaningful work. People are waiting around for the perfect job or taking a job only if it's what they're most passionate about. Working toward your passions is a great goal, and in a perfect world we would all be making money by following our dreams. But that's just not reality.

Don't get me wrong—all of us should strive to do what we love, or at least make progress toward that goal. But until then, we can learn to adjust our mind-set. When you're in a job you don't love, remember that your job doesn't define you, but *how* you do your job can.

To engage in a retire-while-you-work mind-set, frame your work in a meaningful way instead of constantly searching for meaningful work.

To engage in a retire-while-you-work mind-set, frame your work in a meaningful way instead of constantly searching for meaningful work. So even if you're not passionate about your work, you can be passionate about *how* you do your work. Taking pride in what you do can immediately increase your enjoyment and satisfaction while you're at the office.

You can also be passionate about how your work provides for other aspects of your life. Appreciate every dollar that comes in, and use it to enjoy life. For instance, save up your hard-earned cash to take vacations, pay off your mortgage, or save for your kid's college education.

Think of your job as a means to an end. If you have something you're passionate about, use your job as a fundraiser for your dreams (I like that saying ... did I just come up with that?). Invest in a side hustle you're excited to do on the weekends. Or pay off all your debts and your mortgage with your current job so you can transition to another job that may not come with as hefty of a paycheck later on in life. Relieve some of the financial pressure today so you can take a stab at that dream job tomorrow.

Stop worrying about finding that perfect love-everything-about-it job. Instead, make the job you have today work for you now. It's possible. I've seen many people get to this place just by changing their mind-set and reframing what their job represents. And guess what? Most clients I've seen end up finding the path to that dream job, thanks to a positive, healthy frame of mind. We are the energy we put out into the universe.

2. FIND CONGRUENCIES IN YOUR PRIORITIES.

Our calendars and finances don't lie. If you look at how you spend your time and money, you'll see exactly where your priorities are.

Where are you putting your time and resources? Are your days filled with client meetings and dinners? If so, chances are, you highly value your job. Are your days filled with morning workout sessions, lunchtime runs, and pickup games at night? Then you probably place fitness as a top priority. If you see lots of playdates, preschool interviews, and parenting classes on your calendar, family is your top priority.

The problem arises when we say *X* is a priority, but our resources, time, energy, and money are spent on *Y*. To be successful and find fulfillment in life, you've got to make sure that your dreams and goals are congruent with your day-to-day activities.

For example, no matter how much you believe that family is the most important part of life, if your calendar is filled with endless business meetings and your money and nights are spent with friends, there's no way your family life is thriving. Spend your time and energy on what you value most.

If your goals and activities aren't congruent, step back and figure out what needs to change. Maybe you need to reorganize your priorities or understand what you want out of life. Then set up your life so that your activities are congruent with those priorities.

Daily practice leads to accomplishment. So whatever you value, put it into practice today, tomorrow, the next day, and the day after.

3. LEARN SELF-CARE.

The following statement is one you'll recognize, but read it carefully: "Should the cabin experience sudden pressure loss, stay calm and listen for instructions from the cabin crew. If you are traveling with children or someone who requires assistance, secure your mask first and then assist the other person."

We hear this safety demonstration at the beginning of every flight, but we probably don't realize how it applies to our daily lives. One of the most dangerous beliefs out there is that we need to take care of others before we take care of ourselves. Although that ideology stems from a good place, it's not a healthy one to live by.

Think about it—if you're fumbling to help your kid or parent wear their oxygen mask before putting on your own, you risk jeopardizing your own well-being and, therefore ultimately, your ability to help the other person. All too often, we burn ourselves out for the sake of helping everyone else around us—be it coworkers, friends, kids, partners, parents, or someone else. How you're impacted will also impact the people around you. If you're feeling down, the people around you will inevitably feel that sadness, too. If you're worn out, you won't have the energy to help others in the ways they need. If you're lacking emotionally, physically, or spiritually within yourself, you'll have nothing to pull from to help others.

True caring comes from abundance. Instead of expending ourselves by constantly putting everyone else's needs first, we need to practice self-care. If you're full of energy, joy, and self-love, it will be easy to draw for others from the deep well of abundance you've created within yourself.

Taking care of yourself can look different for everyone, but mostly it involves setting healthy boundaries, learning to say no, and understanding your own needs. It can even come down to building healthy lifestyle habits. If you're taking care of yourself emotionally, you should also be taking care of yourself physically. Set goals to exercise more, eat healthier, get into bed at a decent hour, and find ways to keep your creativity alive. I used to think doing this was entirely selfish, but once you realize you can't love or help others until you love and help yourself, that myth goes away.

Whatever it looks like for you, make sure you're putting your proverbial oxygen mask on first before helping the person next to you.

4. FIND PEOPLE TO HELP YOU.

Surrounding yourself with positive people who can encourage and support you during your career and in your personal life is a major asset many people disregard. Whether it's a community group through your church, friends who keep you accountable, or a mentor, I highly suggest finding like-minded people to connect with.

I can't tell you how essential my time with my mentors and counselors was, and still is, today. Without their knowledge and wisdom, it would have taken me much longer to understand what I was missing in life. My immaturity and shame used to tell me that seeking any type of help meant I was broken, weak, and incapable of being strong. But that's a superficial and shallow mind-set. Working with a mentor was one of the best things I've ever done.

In my experience, a mentor is someone who, through life experiences, has accumulated a level of wisdom you could greatly benefit from when navigating your own set of life experiences, struggles, and pain. I met my mentor, George, about six years ago. He materialized right before chaos broke out in my life and has been by my side through everything imaginable: divorce; a major job transition; the launching of my own private firm; my learning to date and love again (still learning); my getting through a two-year contract lawsuit with a former employer; my growth in my relationship with God; and my learning to be a better son, boss, future husband, and father.

My mentor has also taught me what it means to be a mentee—how to listen, learn, and grow into a mentor for others based on the wisdom he's shared and the depth of experiences we've navigated together. He's helped me see that life is not a sprint to the end; it's a lifelong process to self-betterment. It's a constant pursuit and quest for knowledge.

George, I love you, and not a day goes by that I'm not grateful you came into my life when I needed you most. Even more so, I appreciate you for teaching me how to become a mentor for others so I can keep paying it forward.

Our firm's mission statement is, "Helping restore vital balance and financial strength through life's many transitions." We've learned over the years that all of us—no exceptions—need a team of people around us during major changes, whether its divorce, marriage, the sale of a business, or the loss of a loved one. Don't try and be a hero and do it alone—I've yet to see that plan work well. Seek a mentor—the difference you'll see in your personal and professional lives will be remarkable.

5. HAVE A PLAN: THE THREE-BUCKET PRINCIPLE

With any client who comes into my office, I like to start off talking about what I call the *three buckets of money*. It doesn't matter whether they have $10 million in the bank, are just getting started on a financial plan, or are right out of college. In my opinion, everyone should be working toward having their three buckets set up. Once you understand what the buckets represent, it's an incredibly easy system to follow. The concept is very simple, and it helps make a complicated financial world and the stock market seem much more comprehensible and visual. After years of trying every method under the sun to get my points across to clients, this concept has been, by far, the ticket to helping improve my clients' financial situations.

The world of money and investing can get overwhelming (and boring) very quickly. I've been to nothing short of one hundred investment conferences and seminars. And at the end of the day, keeping it simple absolutely works. The three buckets are the foundation of what I believe to be the essence of a retire-while-you-work, lifetime, fluid financial plan.

Chapter 4 covers the three buckets of money in detail—get excited!

TEN THOUSAND DAYS

Being the numbers nerd I am, one day I was sitting there thinking, okay, I'm almost forty, so how many more days do I have until I'm seventy?

I figured it had to be at least 100,000 days. Doing some quick math, I realized it was closer to 10,000 (10,970 days to be exact). Now, to you this might not be exciting or surprising or evoke the same level of emotion as it did for me.

I thought about those 10,000 days and compared them to dollars. If each day were worth a dollar, the number of dollars I'd have by the time I reached my older years were much more limited than I'd imagined. I would have only $10,000 if I lived every day from today until age seventy. Wow!

I don't mean to be depressing by any means, but here's what that revelation meant to me. We always hear that life is short, but it's never seemed that way to me. Yes, time goes by fast, but thirty years from now seems very distant and out of reach. When I realized how limited our days are, the idea of working for tomorrow started to appear foolish. Why waste any days if they're so limited? For example, if we spent ten years being miserable and plugging away so we could live later, we just wasted 3,650 days.

While it may not always be possible to live every day like you're dying (a Tim McGraw song reference), it *is* possible to reframe how you treat each day. All of a sudden, the stakes are too high to waste days not pursuing your passion and dreams. I know I'm working hard to stop making decisions centered around how they'll impact me later. Instead, I focus on considering the immediate gratification an activity will bring.

Of course, like anything else, we have to balance today with tomorrow. I encourage you to listen to your gut and quit saying, *One day I'll go for it.* The time is now. Or at least this year. At a minimum, you can start planning and laying the groundwork for that big move you've been hoping to make for years. Create a vision board. My dear friend, Carly, has been coaching and working with me for the last few years on dreaming big. I cannot say enough about what just the process of doing this exercise will unlock inside of you.

But what about the risk, David? What if I fail? Hockey Hall of Famer Wayne Gretzky said, "You miss one hundred percent of the shots you don't take." So your biggest risk isn't the possibility of failure; your true risk is not trying. If you don't pursue dreams, you won't achieve what your soul craves.

FULFILLING YOUR DREAMS

I encourage clients to follow their dreams, especially those long-held dreams, even if they're far from being uber-wealthy. I'll give you an example. Let's say there's a woman named Betty, a sweet old lady who lives in Small Town, Tennessee. Betty has a couple hundred thousand bucks in her IRA and retirement accounts, and she lives off Social Security. She lives modestly but is happy as a clam in retirement—all she requires is about $1,000 a month from her account to pay bills.

Now, Betty wants to take her eight grandchildren to Disney World, an expensive trip. It's her life's dream to spoil them. Rather than lecture her on why that's a bad idea, I'm of the opinion that sometimes—in fact, most times—dreams are worth the investment. Here's the advice I'd give Betty.

"Betty, you've worked so hard your whole life for this money. You're in your seventies. What are we waiting for? You have great health, you exercise, and your grandkids are at the ages where they can enjoy Disney. When you pass, what else are you going to do with that money? You cannot replace this experience. Those kids will talk about this trip for years and years—they'll never forget. You're going to have that as a legacy."

I'm closing my eyes—and I can see it now. Betty hugs me; it's liberating for her to hear this. She goes on the trip and sends pictures. After she gets back, she looks like a different person—she's proud and happy. She even carries herself differently. But you know what? She doesn't talk about the money even once. It never comes up.

Finally, about six months later, we reflect on it again in a meeting. Every time she comes in, she thanks me, even though I explain that she only has herself to thank—she's the one who worked for her money. I was just there to help her find her *why* and help her make it happen. She tells us she's never for a moment regretted taking that trip. It was scary to her at the time, but she said it ended up being the best thing she ever did.

Betty explains that her initial perception was that I'd discourage her from taking her dream vacation with her grandkids—just another indication that our industry is broken. People think they have to give us their money and then fear asking to use some of it. It's a guilt-based brokenness. How backward is that?

Seeing how happy clients are when they accomplish whatever it is they set out to achieve is what keeps me coming back into the office every day. When you can help make a difference in somebody's life, when you help them get unstuck, when their mind is telling them no and they're fearful, but then you help free them of it and encourage them to live their dreams, there's nothing like it.

Now, I'm not suggesting we throw financial plans to the wind, be irresponsible, and let people like Betty spend all their money. It's about balance and evaluating the entire financial picture.

I could have advised Betty to hoard that $15,000, and the stock market could have swallowed it whole in a single stroke of bad luck. What a shame it would have been for Betty to die at eighty and regret never having taken her grandkids to Disney. With a plan, it's possible to live the retire-while-you-work mentality into retirement.

> We can't take money with us when we go, but the experiences and memories we create with it will last forever and for generations.

Examples like Betty and my dad motivate me.

We can't take money with us when we go, but the experiences and memories we create with it will last forever and for generations. And they're a much more meaningful, powerful legacy than money. You may not want to die bouncing your last check (like my client), but instead of leaving a million dollars and no memories to your heirs, why not leave $100,000 and a lifetime of smiles and memories? *Balance.*

CHAPTER 4

THE THREE BUCKETS OF MONEY

The concept of the three buckets is the big one. If we can get this foundation and formula right together, then you'll have taken a huge step toward retiring while you work. It all starts here, and this concept should be your number one focus, way before considering what types of investments to buy. If a financial planner who starts your meeting discussing investments and products has priorities that are clearly out of whack, run out the door, please.

I've used my three buckets approach since I started my practice, and it resonates with people in a very special and motivating way. After an extensive career helping thousands of individuals and families with their finances, I've never had a single principle resonate so well with every single client, whether they had $50,000 or $50 million to invest.

Most financial ruins I've seen, especially after the 2008 financial crisis, weren't because the stock market dipped; rather, they were because people didn't have the three buckets in place and in the right ratios.

The three buckets are the foundation for retiring while you work.

> **The three buckets are the foundation for retiring while you work. They'll ensure that you're always building your finances in the right direction.**

They ensure that you're always building your finances in the right direction. It doesn't mean you won't go through bad periods in the stock market or face some serious financial pitfalls, but it does mean you'll be prepared and have a plan in place well before these things ever happen. Being prepared is everything, and I tell my clients this every single day.

And now (drum roll, please), here are the three buckets:

BUCKET 1:
Emergency Fund or Cash Bucket

BUCKET 3:
Retirement Bucket

BUCKET 2:
The Middle Bucket (yes, I should patent that creativity)

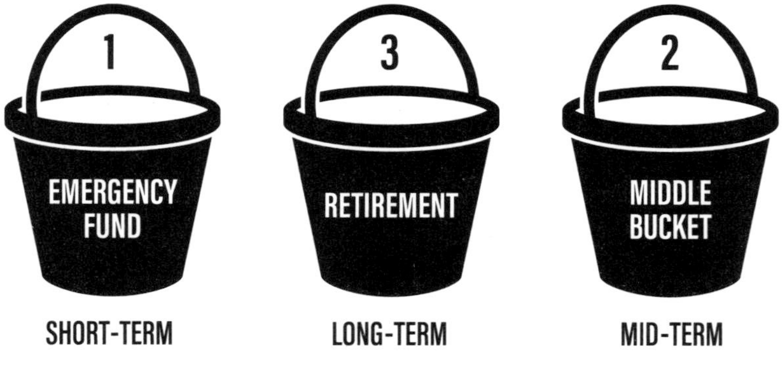

Let's look at each bucket in detail. You'll notice they're not listed in numerical order; there's a reason for that, as you'll find out shortly. (I couldn't make it as easy as one-two-three; it needs to appear a little more complex so I look a little smarter. After all, I spent years leading meetings talking about standard deviations, alpha, beta, turnover ratios, and P/E ratios, watching eyes glaze over and heads loll without fail.)

The three-bucket concept connects us more to our clients, makes it about them, and gets right into what they should be doing.

"People don't care how much you know until they know how much you care." This is our tagline and part of my team's vision. In today's society, I've learned that people just want to know what to do. If they trust you and your intentions, they'll listen. They're coachable, and they're desperate and hungry for the right advice.

BUCKET 1: EMERGENCY FUND

According to *Money* magazine, 78 percent of Americans will face a major negative financial event in any given ten-year period.[11] That doesn't sound very exciting, but Murphy's Law tends to strike every decade or so, which is not necessarily a bad thing if we plan for it in advance. So let's talk about how to do this. I've heard many philosophies over time, but I get the most excited about the following approach to building out this bucket.

Instead of dipping into your regular savings account, or even worse, going into debt to cover yourself during financial events, you'd use Bucket 1. My rule of thumb is to save three to six months' worth of expenses for your emergency fund. When you're calculating the amount for this first bucket, add up your rent or mortgage, bills and utilities, and your basic living expenses, such as food and gas. This could range anywhere from a few thousand dollars to $50,000,

11 "Personal Finance Basics: Negative Events Will Happen To You—Plan Ahead with Insurance and an Emergency Fund," SmartOnMoney, https://www.smartonmoney.com/personal-finance-basics-negative-events-will-happen-to-you-plan-ahead-with-insurance-and-an-emergency-fund/.

depending on your specific needs.

I know those numbers can seem extremely daunting, but don't let them scare you. It can take a few years to get this bucket in place, so just do what you can with the finances you have. Maybe that means saving $100 a month, getting a part-time job, or selling your unused household items on eBay or Craigslist. There is no shame in this game, I can assure you.

Also, keep funds in this account for major purchases you know you'll likely make in the next year. For example, if you plan to buy a car or have a pool installed, keep this money liquid in Bucket 1 so it's not invested in the stock market with up and down fluctuations. This money should be held in a savings or money-market type account.

And yes, while these accounts may be paying near zero ("Point nothing," as I like to say) interest, at least at the time of writing this book, that's okay, because this money is meant to remain stable so it's there when you need it. We have plenty of opportunity for growth investments coming up in Buckets 2 and 3. I always explain to our clients that on a scale of one to ten (one being almost no risk and ten being aggressive and 100 percent invested in the stock market), this account should be a one.

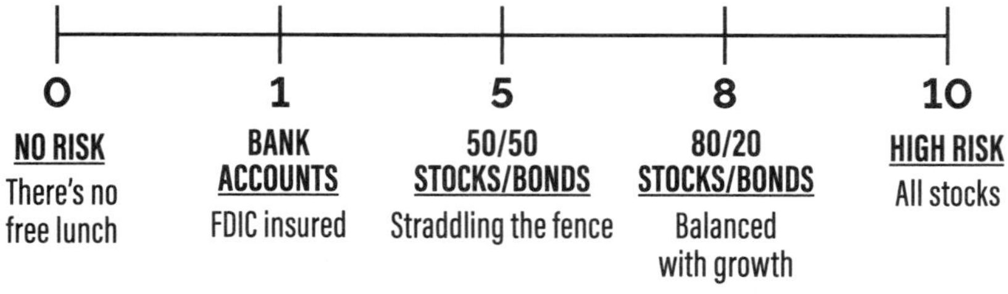

Many of my clients keep one to two years' worth of expenses in this bucket due to the cyclical nature of the industries they work in (such as music and entertainment) and sporadic incomes. Seeing that our office is located in Nashville, Tennessee ("Nash-Vegas," as the magazines call it), a large segment of our client base is composed of songwriters, touring musicians, and athletes. Therefore, it's critical we design a custom Bucket 1 for them based on their specific income flow (think royalties for songwriters, touring schedule for musicians, and season schedule for athletes).

I like to have more money in Bucket 1 for clients in these types of industries, or any business where the largest compensation comes from commissions or sales bonuses (e.g., real estate agents, medical sales, etc.) that can fluctuate with economic conditions, unlike compensation received from a W-2 salary.

I go into greater detail on this concept in part 2 of this book, my Q&A section.

It doesn't matter how much you save at first or for how long. The key is to commit to building a plan that can give you the financial opportunity and ability to focus on everything else I've mentioned so far and the items I'm about to discuss. As soon as this bucket is set, you can move on to the other two. But when explaining this principle to clients, I always jump ahead to Bucket 3 next, so here we go …

BUCKET 3: RETIREMENT BUCKET

Bucket 3 is where you save for retirement. The initial response I get in many meetings or on my radio show is, *But David, I thought the idea was to retire while I work, not save all my money for when I'm older and can't really enjoy it.* You're absolutely right—we're not going to over-save into this bucket and ignore the journey along the way. No way.

But we do want to have a balanced amount in this bucket for later in life because there are specific tax advantages in doing so. Plus, you'll have access to this money typically at age fifty-nine-and-a-half (don't ask me how the IRS came up with fifty-nine-and-a-half years old). With people living much longer these days, that's still young! So stick with me here; Bucket 3 is more exciting than it might initially sound—or at least more important than it first appears.

Once you've calculated your emergency fund and set up Bucket 1, you can start putting 15 to 20 percent of your gross household income toward retirement. Many online articles and advisors suggest putting 10 percent into retirement. Although this is a great start, my years of experience suggest that 20 percent is more likely to get you closer to your goal of retiring while you work.

On the flip side, I also run into clients and articles, and some advisors, who suggest saving 50 percent of your income for retirement. I confidently disagree with this advice because it's likely to cause a huge gap of unhealthy, imbalanced living in the years before age fifty-nine-and-a-half, unless your income is so high that you can save this much and still do all the things your heart desires. If that's the case, please call me to schedule an appointment at six-one-five ... okay, okay, you get it.

If you're lucky enough to be at a company that offers a matching 401(k) plan, put part of your Bucket 3 money there—at least up to the matching contribution. It's free money you shouldn't pass up. In addition to that, or if you don't have a 401(k) option, look into a Roth or traditional IRA. If you're self-employed, consider a SEP IRA or other retirement vehicle. A combination of these tax-efficient vehicles will help develop your Bucket 3. As much as I would love to explain every detail and difference among each of these retirement accounts, I am resisting the urge so we can keep the focus on the big picture and not cause heads to nod, eyes to glaze over, or book reviews to be terrible.

But on a serious note, some of these accounts (traditional IRA and SEP) give you a tax deduction now (as you contribute) and have the potential to grow tax-deferred (meaning you don't pay taxes on gains along the way). But, they're taxed as ordinary income (just like your normal "work" income) when you pull them out after age fifty-nine-and-a-half. And some accounts (such as a Roth IRAs) give you no tax advantage when you contribute (meaning they are after-tax contributions) but have the potential to grow tax free (wait for it) *forever*. Yes, these make my little CPA heart happy.

Each account has different contributing limits, and they all change a little each year. But, as with anything else in financial planning and life, the best plan is balance. That's right—have a mix of each type of retirement account so that when you do get past the (IRS-deemed unusual) age of fifty-nine-and-a-half, you have access to some taxable money and some tax-free money. This gives financial planners a lot of options to build a tax-efficient income stream in the future. I tell clients that my job is to think twenty years ahead for them so they can stay in the present *now*.

Bucket 3 money can be invested in more growth-oriented and aggressive investments than Buckets 1 or 2 because this is your long-term money. I talked about the one-to-ten scale earlier and how Bucket 1 would be a one, meaning as low-risk an investment as possible. I typically suggest Bucket 3 be somewhere between a seven and a ten, depending on the client's appetite for risk, along with their age and account size.

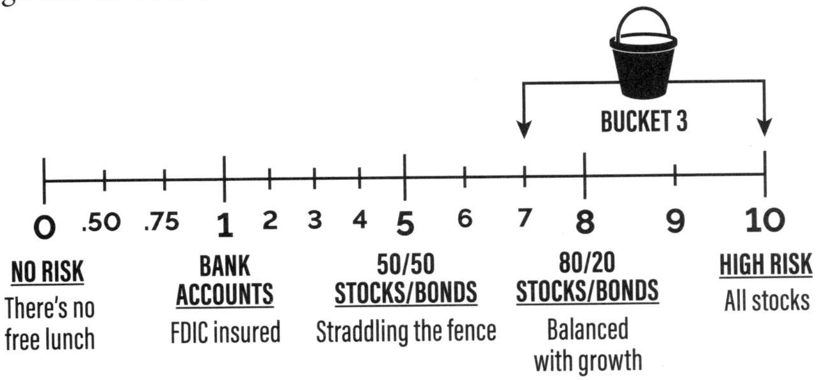

Why does the size of the account matter? I get this question a lot. Before I answer that, let me first say that the age factor is simple—basically, the younger you are, the more time the money has to grow and the less concern there is about the volatility of the stock market. That's why I encourage clients to choose a nine or ten on the risk scale. Then I assess the risk of each client by asking questions. This is more of an art than a science, where I blend the textbook financial planning answer with the emotional answer. If I sense that someone is nervous about the stock market, has had a bad experience with past investments, or appears anxious or nervous in general, I tend to suggest throttling back to the seven range.

Now back to the size question. I must profess I'm a lover of behavioral finance and the human psychology associated with money and investing. I've studied it for more than fifteen years, both academically and professionally as I've come face to face with thousands of people. Here's what I've learned: as account size grows, dips in the stock market hit harder. If you have $30,000 in a 401(k) and it falls 20 percent, you see a loss of $6,000. If you have $2 million in that 401(k), the same percentage drop reveals itself as a $400,000 loss. Gulp. When I use examples like this with clients, I can usually identify their *Uncle point*—the amount of loss that would cause them to call me and say, "Pull the plug. Get me out of the market." Talking real numbers versus percentages of potential loss is very important when it comes to figuring out where you fall on the one-to-ten scale.

Let's look at a hypothetical example. John is thirty-seven and his wife, Cindy, is thirty-four. They each have 401(k)s and IRAs in Bucket 3 that they don't plan on touching until they're at least in their sixties. I start by asking them, "On a scale of one to ten, one being all cash and ten being all stocks, where do you think you fall?"

John's eyes light up, and he says, with confidence, "Ten."

I ask him why. He replies, "I'm young, I don't need this money until I'm old, and I love risk."

Cindy says four, because she doesn't like losing money and because her father lost half his retirement in the stock market. She'll never forget that.

After having an in-depth talk with our team about risk, expectations of returns (real numbers, not just percentages), downside volatility, previous experiences, and emotions, we determine that John's account should be a nine and Cindy's a seven. John's moved down from his initial answer, based on my explanation that you don't get much more long-term return by having 100 percent stocks versus having 90 percent stocks with a 10 percent padding in bonds.

Cindy was able to move up to a seven after we decided together to add a little extra money to Bucket 1 so she would be less likely to worry about and watch Bucket 3. I showed her how seven to ten was the ideal risk level for this bucket, and how she would fall at the lower end, which gave her some relief. By adding some cash to her safety net, I was simply listening to her needs and accommodating her emotions so she could have the highest shot at meeting her long-term goals without living in constant panic, watching the ticker at the bottom of MSNBC.

This is why I *love* my job. The art of financial planning is not just choosing the right investment products and mix, but more about being a good listener and understanding investor psychology. At the end of the day, you can build the best investment portfolio, but if your clients don't feel comfortable and understand the bucket philosophy, research shows they'll derail and make wrong decisions at the worst times. Personal finance is 80 percent personal, and 20 percent finance.

BUCKET 2: THE MIDDLE BUCKET

Last but not least, let's talk about Bucket 2. I save this bucket for last because most people don't have Buckets 1 and 3 set up correctly, and it's critical to get those in order before we get ahead of ourselves. Bucket 2 is where you put money for all of life's midterm goals. I like to call this the *retire-while-you-work bucket*. You can probably guess that this is my favorite bucket.

Bucket 2 is money you're saving for your kid's college, a down payment on a house, a rental property, or for your home mortgage loan to pay it off more quickly. When clients come in and ask where they should put new money, I ask them two questions: (1) "Do you still have Bucket 1 filled with at least six months' worth of income?" and (2) "Have you been putting at least 15-20 percent of your earnings into Bucket 3?"

If they answer yes to both questions, then my advice is that anything extra can go into Bucket 2. This bucket can hold as much disposable income as you want. Simple, right?

The fun part about Bucket 2 is that we start simple, but then over the years add many layers to diversify and make our clients' balance sheets interesting. For starters, let's say a client has a fully funded emergency fund and is actively saving for retirement. She comes to my office explaining that she has an extra $300,000 in her checking account (from selling a rental property, inheritance, etc.). The first thing we would do is open a regular (meaning, nonretirement, known as retail or taxable) investment account in which we would build a portfolio that is accessible and liquid, should she need it in the coming years. It's important to have access to money outside of Bucket 1 in case you ever exhaust your emergency fund (for example, losing your job, having your car break down, and needing a new HVAC unit in the same month).

The investment account in Bucket 2 can be subdivided into multiple accounts with different purposes. For example, I always recommend that clients open accounts to save for their kids' education costs. Typically, I suggest the 529 account[12] to save money tax-free toward college, which allows the parent or custodian to retain control of the money. This advice, of course, varies, and rules change from time to time.

It's also best practice to come up with a monthly amount you can save into the investment account in Bucket 2—such as your children's college savings account—and toward paying down your mortgage. This is where I love the hybrid approach—putting some money each month toward each of these goals within Bucket 2. For example, if a client tells me he can put $4,000 per month toward Bucket 2 (assuming he has Buckets 1 and Bucket 3 on track), I would come up with a formula that allows us to save in each of these areas. It might look something like this:

- Put $2,000 per month into the investment account to keep building momentum and dollar-cost averaging[13] into the market (meaning that you buy at different points as it goes up and down).
- Pay down an extra $1,000 per month on the house, accelerating the payoff period.

---

12 The 529 account is a tax-advantaged account designed to help save for future education costs. Contributions have the potential to grow tax-deferred, and qualified withdrawals are tax-free. States sponsor their own 529 plans, which may offer additional tax benefits for in-state residents. As with other investments, there are generally fees and expenses associated with participation in a 529 plan. There is also a risk that these plans may lose money or not perform well enough to cover college costs as anticipated. Investors should carefully consider the investment objectives, risks, charges, and expenses associated with 529 plans before investing. This and other information about 529 plans is available in the issuer's official statement and should be read carefully before investing.

13 Dollar-cost averaging is a method of investing fixed amounts on a regular schedule as a means to help reduce investment risk. Dollar-cost averaging cannot guarantee a profit or protect against loss, and you should consider your financial ability to continue purchases through periods of low price levels.

- Add $500 per month into each of the two kids' 529 college accounts while they're young, to really build momentum.

> **As you can see, the point is to build each of the investment accounts while paying down debt so your money is always working in the right direction for you.**

As you can see, the point is to build each of the investment accounts while paying down debt so your money is always working in the right direction for you. I use this same approach for additional funds and lump sums that become available to clients to invest. This means that if they receive a $50,000 commission at work, I would allocate this money in a similar way as I did the monthly contribution amounts above. It might look something like this:

- The client has a goal of taking a family vacation after the next bonus. Take $10,000 to enjoy precious time with family (important in the retire-while-you-work philosophy).
- Add $10,000 to the investment account in Bucket 2.
- Put an additional $5,000 in both children's 529 savings while they're young to jumpstart compounding and growth.
- Pay down $20,000 on the house because only $100,000 is outstanding and the client desires to pay it off quickly (without ignoring other parts of the plan).

In the example above, a hybrid approach allows for family time, investment in Bucket 2, progress on the kids' college savings, and funds to chip away at the remaining home mortgage. With every client, the actual dollar amounts will vary. The important part is having this conversation together and balancing out Bucket 2.

Back to my one-to-ten investment risk scale. I usually tell clients a level five or six makes the most sense here—what I call straddling the fence—with maybe 50/50 stocks to bonds where we're aiming at a decent return if the market's up, but also having half of the money in fixed income as a buffer. The reason we want to be less aggressive here is the likelihood of you using money from Bucket 2 is (and should be) much higher than you tapping into retirement Bucket 3, due to taxes and potential early withdrawal penalties.

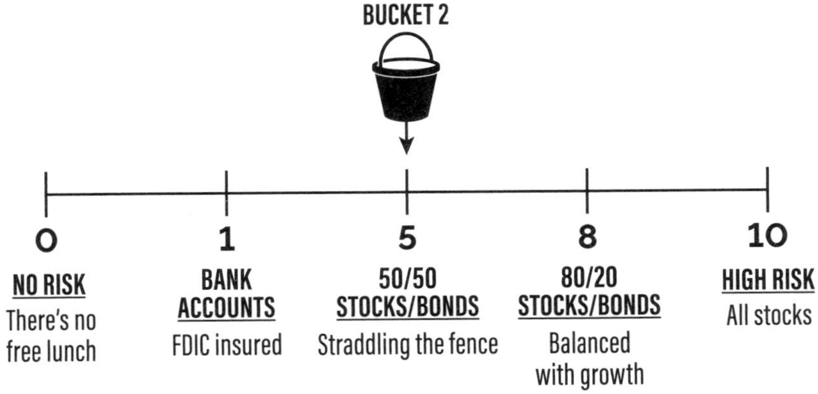

After you build this investment account in Bucket 2, get some momentum in college savings, and get the home mortgage down quite a bit, you can start adding additional layers. This is where you can add some rental properties, if that's something you want to do. I love real estate but I also realize I don't want to spend all my time managing properties.[14] It's all about balance and diversification.

My best advice for buying investment real estate is to make sure you always put at least 25 percent down. Sure, you can do less and get approved for a loan, but this helps ensure a good cushion of equity in case of a market downturn. Rental properties can provide passive income and be a nice addition to this middle bucket. And over time,

14 In addition to the time requirements, rental properties also have additional risks that are specific to investing in real estate.

as you pay off the properties, you can build up a nice monthly income to help fund your retire-while-you-work goals.

Clients often ask me, "How do we look at the equity in our home? Is that part of Bucket 2?" I usually exclude the equity in your primary residence for planning purposes, because we always need a home to live in. Even if you sold your house, more than likely you'll use that equity to buy another one. The reality is that if you buy a $500,000 home and it appreciates to $1 million, then yes, you have $500,000 of equity. But if you sell that home and want something similar, more than likely you'll spend $1 million to get the next place—unless you're moving to a lower-cost real estate market or city, or plan to significantly downsize.

On the flip side, if you end up having to sell your home at a loss, more than likely it's because the market isn't good, meaning that, consequently, you'll be able to buy your next home a little cheaper. Remember, the key is to own a home so you're "in the game," as they say, and keeping up with the market. Many people rent for so many years that by the time they're ready to buy, the market has become unaffordable, and they wish they'd committed earlier.

We often work with clients who are looking to make a change in their lifestyle and want to retire while they work. Here's a typical scenario that involves a fairly successful couple in their forties who have built up quite a bit of equity in their home:

Both individuals are doctors with great income, but they feel like life's passing them by because they work eighty or more hours a week with no time for travel, which is their passion. They've saved around $2 million in investments through their financial planner and purchased a home for around $600,000 that's now worth $900,000 (thanks to the Nashville "boom"), and they owe around $400,000 on it. They decide to sell their home and purchase a condo for $350,000.

This frees up around $150,000 after they pay off the condo.

In this hypothetical example, I would have them take the $150,000 and put it in Bucket 1 to give them three years' worth of a travel budget and fill in the gaps with income, since they've both decided to go part-time and make around one-third of their normal salaries. This decision allows them to retire while they work, live a smaller and simpler footprint, travel the world, and still keep their minds active with work, having the option to go back full-time if they ever decide to.

I've seen many situations just like this—and it's been amazing to watch our clients' journeys!

Establishing these three buckets helps provide funds for an unexpected event, savings for midterm life goals, and a nest egg for income in early retirement, which is the entire concept of retiring while you work.

Establishing these three buckets helps provide funds for an unexpected event, savings for midterm life goals, and a nest egg for income in early retirement, which is the entire concept of retiring while you work.

Over the past fifteen years, nearly every catastrophic financial situation I've witnessed could've been prevented by having this basic balance among the buckets. Here is just one example of the types of scenarios I experienced during the 2008 meltdown:

A hypothetical client panics after he loses his job during the financial crisis—he doesn't have any savings in Bucket 1 or investments in Bucket 2. He withdraws $200,000 from his 401(k) out of fear while the market is down 40 percent and also pays early withdrawal penalties because he isn't fifty-nine-and-a-half yet. The $200,000 he pulls out, after 25 percent taxes and a 10 percent penalty, nets out to around $130,000. The client has now pushed retirement back another five years. Painful to watch, but fairly easy to avoid with good planning and the bucket strategy.

I believe that a good life can be yours. You don't have to be a victim of debt, fear, stress, or an unfulfilling job.

Think about answers to these questions: What do you want to do with your life? How can your current job help you reach your goals? How can you take better care of yourself so you can care for others?

If you put in the work and set goals, the burden of your financial fears will lighten as you retire while you work.

I believe in this way of life with all my heart. It's a life of freedom, joy, and fulfillment that's just waiting for you. Don't save all of life's pleasures for retirement. Now is the time to enjoy life. Now is the time to find purpose. Now is the time to live.

PART 2

RETIRE WHILE YOU WORK

ANSWERS TO COMMONLY ASKED QUESTIONS

This second part addresses questions people commonly ask me which reflect the retire-while-you-work philosophy.

This is not a cookie-cutter approach; this is my personal approach—one I've developed as a result of my own experiences and by helping thousands of people build their financial plans. In fifteen years, I've used these strategies with tons of clients, regardless of their income level, age, or net worth.

Each response to the upcoming questions should be read through the lens of the new way of thinking about money. While many timeless principles still make sense and hold true today, much of this industry's ways are broken, antiquated, and due a renovation.

I have my tool belt on—let's do this!

CHAPTER 5

HOW MUCH CASH SHOULD I HAVE?

The amount of cash you should have liquid is all about Bucket 1—the emergency funds bucket. Again, I recommend clients have enough to cover three to six months' worth of expenses in the emergency fund. That's a generic starting point.

Clients who have sporadic income, such as musicians and songwriters, need to have more cash in this bucket—enough to cover six to twelve months' worth of expenses—because they're reliant on fluctuating royalties versus a steady paycheck.

Clients who have a smaller base salary but who receive big bonuses quarterly should also hold more cash in Bucket 1. Because if they were to lose their jobs, it's difficult to predict how much they'd need.

For retirees, I often recommend bumping the recommended amount of cash in Bucket 1 to one to two years' worth of expenses. What this really means is one to two years of *supplemental* income. For example, if a couple needs $100,000 a year to live on, and they already have $30,000 coming in each year from Social Security and $20,000 from a pension, they have $50,000 of that $100,000 covered. So I'd advise them to have somewhere between $50,000 and $100,000 in cash—$50,000 to cover the gap between their guaranteed fixed income and expenses, plus ideally a second year's worth of expenses, just to be safe.

There are few financial principles I'm more sold on than this one—filling up Bucket 1. Although it might seem boring, doing so is absolutely critical. So please put a big smile on my face by following through and then telling me about it. I'll never grow tired of hearing from people who do!

DON'T LET EMERGENCIES DRAIN YOUR INVESTMENTS.

Clients often ask me, "Why do we need to have so much cash? What's it for?"

The answer? It's for everyday emergencies.

Imagine it being a scorching ninety-seven-degree day in July and both of your HVAC units go out at the same time. It could cost $16,000 to replace them—an expense you weren't planning for. If you're a homeowner, that kind of thing can (and will, at some point) happen.

Or imagine driving and getting hit by an uninsured driver. If you have a high-deductible auto insurance plan because you're trying to save money on the premium, your deductible could be $5,000. Not to mention the added expense of medical bills on top of that.

The purpose of this emergency fund is to make sure you're not having to yank money from Bucket 3 or Bucket 2 to cover an emergency. And we certainly don't want you to go backward in your savings plan by adding large purchases to credit cards or taking equity out of a home you've worked hard to pay down. Having cash in this first bucket can prevent a lot, if not all, of that.

ADD MONEY FOR KNOWN MAJOR EXPENSES TO BUCKET 1.

In addition to having three to six months' or six to twelve months' (depending on your situation) worth of funds set aside in Bucket 1, you should also have money for major expenses you're anticipating in the upcoming year. We don't want money earmarked for shorter-term, big-ticket purchases sitting in Bucket 2 or 3 where it could lose value in a 2008 type of financial crisis. It needs to be in a savings account.

Maybe you plan to buy a $25,000 car for your spouse six months from now. Or maybe you want to build a deck in your backyard or renovate the master bathroom. Add these costs to the funds you calculated to set aside for Bucket 1.

Let's say you need $5,000 a month to keep the lights on, the kids fed, and the mortgage paid. Six months of emergency expenses would be $30,000. So you put $30,000 in one account and name it "Emergency Fund." In addition, you'd set aside money for the master bathroom renovation, which might cost $50,000. If you know you'll be taking a trip that'll cost $10,000 or $20,000, you'll add that money to this account, too. And maybe you have kids in college or in a private high school, and you know it will cost $15,000 for the next year. That money goes in this account, too. And finally, if you have a sporadic and/or 1099 income, set aside money for your quarterly taxes in this account. A good benchmark for this tax expense is 30 percent of your income.

All this money should be in cash form or in a savings account. It's important to have it set aside liquid.

If you receive 1099 income, I recommend putting away 30 percent of every $1 of income you earn so you can pay your federal and state taxes. The last thing you want is April 15 to sneak up on you as you scramble to find enough money to pay your previous year's federal and state income tax.

You don't want this money in the wrong bucket, tied up in the stock market, potentially experiencing steep decreases in value should (or better said, when) we enter another recession.

THE "SLEEP AT NIGHT" NUMBER

Some clients have a "sleep at night" number in their heads—in other words, an amount they want to save that will ease their worries about the future. For instance, they want $100,000 in the bank because it makes them feel safe.

That's definitely okay, because the emotional side of this business and having peace of mind are just as important as the textbook financial answer to what a person's emergency fund should look like. I want to make sure, though, that clients are not setting sleep-at-night money aside out of fear. If they're doing it for peace of mind, that's fine. But if they're setting it aside in cash because they're afraid of having their money in Buckets 2 and 3, all it means is that they're hoarding cash.

I've had clients in the past, many of them older, who had a Great Depression mentality. They were afraid of banks and didn't trust them, so they'd stash $20,000 under their mattresses. One client actually had $40,000 stuffed into a boot (surprise, surprise, being in Nashville) that he'd buried in the backyard. That was just a product of how he was brought up—believing that he couldn't trust the system. There are some extreme approaches out there to safeguarding money, simply because we're all a product of our upbringing and life experiences. That's okay, it's what makes us all unique.

We have to strike the right balance, however, between having money that's liquid and easily accessible for emergencies and having money that's growing as much as it can in investment accounts. We want you to sleep well at night *and* have all your buckets filled appropriately.

I understand where fear comes in—money can be scary. But fear is the enemy of proper planning. As a financial advisor, I always work with clients to find out where that fear stems from so we can address it and move forward. Many times, it originates from a lack of knowledge about proper planning. Other times, we adopt other people's fears that we've been exposed to. It's important to speak with your financial professional about these concerns and make sure you're heard—I cannot stress this enough.

I understand where fear comes in—money can be scary. But fear is the enemy of proper planning.

DON'T LET GREED OUTWEIGH REASON.

Just as fear is a dangerous emotion when it comes to financial planning, greed is dangerous, too. As financial planners, we watch for this powerful and destructive emotion. Greed often kicks in during periods of market increases and low volatility, similar to what we saw in 2017, when the market just seemed to keep going up. In fact, 2017 was the only year since 1990 that the S&P 500 saw twelve months of positive returns.[15]

Clients will ask me, "David, why would I put all this money in cash, making nothing at the bank, when interest rates are so low, and I can potentially increase the worth of my portfolio by 20 percent?"

I have to remind them about 2008 and give them all the statistics. One is that, in an average year, the stock market typically has at least one 10 to 15 percent correction, even during a bull (rising) market. Then every seven to ten years or so, there's a recession, which is a bear market, and it can last two, three, or four years. It's important to remember those down times because when we have periods of growth, everybody forgets about volatility, especially when it hasn't happened for seven to ten years. There's something about that period that makes people forget.

The market is erratic. It's unpredictable, especially during short periods of time. It's more predictable over longer periods. That's why it's important we build a long-term plan—so that we don't react emotionally during periods when the market is behaving like a bad toddler, which it often does.

This is why we have to remember the purpose of Bucket 1 is not to generate a high return. In fact, it's not about the return at all. It's about stability, period. That's the purpose. I can understand people wanting to get the best rate possible. Maybe there's a 1 percent CD or a teaser rate you can get at your local bank. Fine, great. Go do that, but that's not what we're focused on with the emergency fund.

---

15 Anthony Mirhaydari, "Can 2018 Possibly Match Wall Street's Perfect 2017?" CNN MoneyWatch, January 1, 2018, https://www.cbsnews.com/news/can-stock-market-in-2018-possibly-match-perfect-2017/. *The S&P 500 is an index of 500 large capitalization stocks that is widely seen as being representative of the overall US stock market. The S&P 500 is unmanaged and cannot be invested into directly.*

If you're fortunate enough to not have to use Bucket 1 for many years, that's wonderful. But you *will* at some point, and you'll thank your financial advisor for holding you to it. I've seen this so many times—clients who didn't have to use their emergency fund for a long time and had maybe $80,000 in Bucket 1. But then Murphy's Law happened, and they finally needed that money. The entire time, they were telling me, "David, I could be making 20 percent on this money."

Again and again, I would tell them stories of other clients in similar situations. They didn't think they needed the money, either, but then they'd have a health scare, a major malfunction of something in their home, or a child who was in need. These stories usually stop the line of questioning and keep clients focused on the end game.

Don't let greed outweigh reason. Resist the temptation to take money out of your emergency fund to invest it. And that's coming from someone (me) who gets paid on the money you've invested—not on all that money sitting at your bank.

SET ASIDE MONEY FOR HEALTH-CARE.

As people age, sometimes the "wheels start to fall off," and they start experiencing health problems. You have to be prepared for that possibility.

The deductible for your health insurance plan is an obvious expense. It's no secret that deductibles are going up, and health insurance plans are nowhere near as lucrative as they used to be. You especially need to plan ahead if you've chosen a high-deductible plan to keep your premiums down.

Also, be sure to set aside money for any procedures you might need in the next year—a colonoscopy if you're over the age of fifty, for example—because some procedures aren't covered entirely by health insurance.

It's especially important to set money aside for health-care if you're retired and living on Medicare, even if you have a Medicare supplement. Although Medicare does cover a wide range of services for retirees who are sixty-five or older, there are numerous services it won't pay for, such as routine dental visits, vision exams, hearing aids, and long-term care. According to Kiplinger, retirees with health coverage tend to spend approximately $5,000 a year on Medicare, premiums, and other expenses.[16]

When people tell me they need only $50,000 a year to live on, I ask them, "Are you including health-care in that number?" And they'll reply, "I have Medicare. I'm covered." But research proves they'll need an extra $10,000, so we have to plan for that. Again, if it turns out that they don't need the money they've set aside, that's great.

After college, I worked as a consultant at FedEx—and my health plan was *free*. I didn't have to pay any copays, and I had no out-of-pocket expenses. Fast-forward almost twenty years and health-care is much more expensive. Deductibles have to be reached before insurance even kicks in. And even after that, there is an 80/20 split for most procedures—insurance pays 80 percent, but you still have to pay 20 percent. If you're planning to start a family, chances are you'll still have to pay something out of pocket for the delivery of your newborn. So, even if you're young, you need to have money set aside for health-care. You can use a health savings account, which is a tax-efficient way to save, or you can simply save this money in Bucket 1, as part of your emergency fund.

16 Jane Bennett Clark, "How Much You Really Need to Retire," *Kiplinger's Personal Finance*, October 2014, https://www.kiplinger.com/article/retirement/T047-C000-S002-how-much-you-need-to-retire.html.

DON'T LET THIS HAPPEN TO YOU.

When an emergency strikes, it's stressful enough dealing with the emergency itself. It's much worse when you have no money saved for it.

Let's say we're working with a home builder and developer. On paper, he has a net worth of $30 million with all his real estate. But he has only $50,000 in Bucket 1 and $1 million in Bucket 2, liquid. Although that sounds like a lot of money, it's a low percentage of his total net worth—a low percentage of liquid assets compared to what he has in illiquid assets and real estate.

Let's assume he's not worried about it. That's when I'd step in and have a talk, because it's critical for John to have more money in his emergency fund so he can have more balance in liquid assets. For instance, what if a big market correction happens and all of the loans on his properties come due at once? John could quickly find himself underwater.

In this scenario, I'd encourage John to increase Buckets 1 and 2 to a total of $5 million and reduce his real estate holdings to $25 million. I would look at all his properties' worst-case-scenario mortgage payments and figure out what it would take to keep them afloat for six to twelve months, in case of a recession.

My hope is that he'd listen. To add drama (who doesn't like a little drama?), let's say he doesn't, and he comes back and tells me, "But I could make so much more building houses than in the stock market! If I'm lucky, I'll make a 10 percent return in the market with that money, but I could make 30 percent in real estate all day long."

Let's assume this took place in 2005. And then 2008 happens. Temporarily, John's net worth, on paper, falls from $30 million to $8 million. That's not much of a sob story; he still has $8 million. But he'd take a huge hit. More than likely, he'd have to liquidate almost all his investments with me to keep all his other properties afloat. Imagine he gets down to one of his biggest properties and is forced to sell it, because if he doesn't, he'll have to start making some even tougher decisions. From the sale, he manages to stay afloat (barely) and the market eventually rebounds.

After circumstances like this, it's easier to have conversations about balancing out buckets with clients like John. In future review meetings, they'll often laugh and say, "Yeah, yeah. I know. Bucket 1, Bucket 2, blah, blah, blah." But now, they're more willing to listen and be prepared. They're more recession-proof for next time.

I preach this example to many of my clients and let them know that my goal, as a financial planner, is not just to earn my fee from their assets. What drives me is my passion to help people have long-term, sustainable, holistic plans.

WHY MY DAD IS MY WORST CLIENT

Now, not everyone has $30 million to worry about. Every client is different, and every client has different needs. I joke with my dad and tell him he's my worst client because he gets nervous and texts me every time the market goes down. Of course, he has free access to me all the time, and of course he's simultaneously my most loved client, too. But one of the things we've struggled with is that he's old-fashioned. If I weren't pushing on him, he'd stuff all his money in Bucket 1 or under a mattress.

The way I've helped him and a lot of clients understand the three buckets is by reminding them that it's okay to let go of some cash for Bucket 1 because Bucket 2 is money that's liquid and accessible. It's money that, typically, I've invested more conservatively. Not as conservatively as it'd be sitting at the bank, but it's also not invested as aggressively as the money in Bucket 3, which is the long-term retirement money.

As mentioned earlier, I often use a scale of one to ten to describe financial risk. So if you have half your money in the stock market and half in fixed income, like bonds, that would be a five. In comparison, the emergency fund is a one. It's all in a bank account.

My dad, conservative as he is, is similar to many of my other clients. I often have to remind them that there's no need to keep huge sums of money at the bank when a much smaller amount will do. For example, if I have a client that has $200,000 in the bank, I may recommend they keep only about $50,000. How did I arrive at that figure? Well, I'd look at their income needs for the next one to two years, taking into account income they have coming in from Social Security and other sources. The gap between their income and their needs for the next year or two is what we'd keep in Bucket 1.

With conservative clients, I explain that this plan is strategic and in line with the retire-while-you-work philosophy. It may take a little extra convincing, but we're often able to persuade them of the wisdom of moving that extra money into Bucket 2 at a level of five on the scale.

Getting back to the example above, the $150,000 we move to Bucket 2 won't fully be placed into riskier investments. Since we'd look to invest it at a level five, half of that money—$75,000—would be invested very conservatively so the client could get to it. And even if the market fell considerably, that money would probably move very little because it's in fixed income. So, this conservative investor, similar to my dad, would have $50,000 in the bank for emergencies, plus $75,000 still very accessible in Bucket 2, and $75,000 in the stock market. On the next page is a diagram that illustrates this.

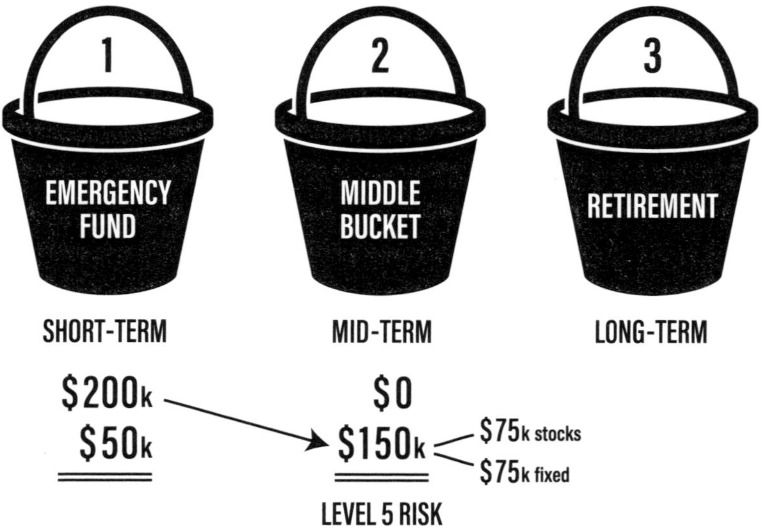

Quite often, when my dad or other conservative investors like him have large sums of money in the bank because that's what they're comfortable with, they really have no foreseeable need to use the entire amount. Many times, they can only envision needing $20,000 to $30,000 all at once, but even if they were to need $100,000, the beauty of how we've distributed the money between Buckets 1 and 2 means they'd have access to that amount without disrupting the money in stocks.

In theory, this means they should never have to lose money by selling stocks when they're down because there's enough liquid available. And at least this way, some of the money in Bucket 2 is hopefully growing and keeping up with, or beating, inflation versus sitting at the bank making zero.

Quite often, my clients, much like my dad, won't follow my advice exactly, but we're usually able to compromise. For instance, instead of going from $200,000 down to just $50,000 in the bank, they might go down to $100,000. But we're still able to get some of the money moved over into the middle bucket.

This is how it is with most clients. Once they realize I'm not trying to push them out of their comfort zone and am simply trying to help them strike a healthy balance between cash, mid-term savings, and long-term/retirement savings, they see the basis for my recommendations.

There is no need to take an insane amount of risk. We take risk in the right buckets, in the right places, and for the right time frames.

EMERGENCY FUND EXAMPLE

To help illustrate how you could go about figuring out how much to keep in Bucket 1, let's pretend I have a client who's a musician; we'll call him Billy. He and his wife—we'll call her Sandy—need $5,000 per month to cover their basic expenses. Billy's income is irregular; it varies based on royalties and whether or not he's touring.

Sandy wants to renovate the kitchen over the next six months, which will likely cost $30,000 based on bids from contractors. Also, their youngest son has just started driving, and they promised him they'd match $5,000 toward the purchase of his car.

So how much money should Billy and Sandy have in their emergency fund? I've chosen to go with twelve months' worth of savings for their emergency fund. Why? Because Billy's a songwriter, meaning his income can be very sporadic. His family's monthly cost is $5,000. Multiply that by twelve and he needs $60,000 in the basic emergency fund.

Add in the $30,000 for the kitchen renovation and $5,000 for their son's car. And because Billy earns income on a 1099 and not a W-2, taxes are not taken out of his checks. We know he'll need to pay $20,000 in taxes for his quarterly tax payments, so that needs to be in the emergency fund, too. And, because he has a high-deductible health plan, we need to set aside $5,000 for health-care expenses. If we add all of that up, it totals $120,000, which is how much Billy and Sandy need in Bucket 1:

Emergency fund for twelve months @ $5,000 per month	$60,000
Kitchen renovation	$30,000
Car for their son	$5,000
Quarterly tax payments	$20,000
Health care expenses	$5,000
Total needed for Bucket 1	**$120,000**

In my experience, I still haven't ever seen a plan go astray if all three of the foundational buckets are set up the right way. Not one time.

CHAPTER 6

SHOULD I PAY OFF MY MORTGAGE?

I get this question almost every week from clients.

I listened to the *Dave Ramsey Show* when I started my career, and I've been a fan of (most of) Dave's advice. He tells people that, to get out of debt, they should pay off their houses first and then start focusing on investing. This is great advice, in my opinion. You can never go wrong being debt-free.

But I believe in more of a hybrid approach, mainly because when you start investing young, your money grows through compounding interest. This is a much wiser option, in my opinion, than spending twenty years putting all your money toward the house but not having much time to put money in growth investments. So I like the approach of making extra payments toward the house while investing simultaneously.

The amount is different for everyone, but here are some guidelines I like to use:

- Before you pay extra on your house, make sure you're contributing to your 401(k) retirement plan at work, if you have one, up to any amount your company may match. That's free money.
- Make sure you have three to six months' worth of income in Bucket 1 for emergency funds.
- After that, if you're able to set up a Roth IRA, you should consider doing that. Make sure you're putting at least 15 percent, but ideally 20 percent, of your income toward retirement.
- Next, start saving money in Bucket 2, the middle bucket. Then you can start tackling your mortgage by making one extra payment a year. That alone can knock down a thirty-year mortgage, typically, five to eight years. And you can expand upon that.

You'll get your foundation right by doing those things, along with some other basic planning items, like having a will and getting an inexpensive term-life insurance policy for your family.

USE EXTRA INCOME TO PAY DOWN YOUR MORTGAGE AND SAVE FOR RETIREMENT.

If your income is high enough and you have your spending under control, then every time you have extra money, put half toward your mortgage and the other half in investments. If you get a $10,000 bonus at work, for example, put $5,000 toward the house for extra principal, and invest the other $5,000.

Now, let's fast-forward ten years. At this point, you should have accrued compounded interest on your investments in Bucket 2. So now, you might be able to pay off the house in twelve years. If you'd put all your extra money toward your mortgage, you might have been able to pay off the house in five to seven years instead of twelve. But because you put some of that money in investments, your overall net worth is likely a lot higher now. You were able to get the same level of appreciation on your house, but you've also saved a bunch of money in retirement and in your middle bucket at the same time.

THE MAGIC OF COMPOUND INTEREST

Keep in mind that it's much harder to start investing later in life and to get the momentum you need. If you start saving at age fifty-five, for example, and tell your financial advisor that you want to retire at sixty-five, that's not a lot of time to build a retirement nest egg. And what if there's a 2008-type of market crash in that small window? It's better to begin early so you have more time on your side.

HERE'S AN EXAMPLE OF WHY YOU CAN'T BEAT LONG-TERM SAVINGS:

Let's look at the long-term investment results achieved by four theoretical investors, each of whom started saving at different times in their careers. This exercise is based on each person investing $10,000 per year at a 6.5 percent annual rate of return. The results are stunning.

INVESTOR 1, who invests a total of $400,000 from ages twenty-five to sixty-five, finishes with $1.9 million in a retirement fund.

INVESTOR 2, who gets a slow start but invests $300,000 from thirty-five to sixty-five, ends up with $919,892—roughly half of Investor 1's take.

INVESTOR 3, who for some reason saved just $100,000 from twenty-five to thirty-five, actually nets more than Investor 2—$950,588.

INVESTOR 4 invests $400,000 from twenty-five to sixty-five but decides to play it incredibly safe, holding cash at 2.25 percent annual. He retires with just $652,214.

But investors don't have to save $10,000 a year to take advantage of compound interest. According to the Motley Fool, if you invested $420 a month with a 7 percent average annual return over a forty-year period, you could ultimately yield $1 million. However, if that number is reduced to 3 percent, which is what a more conservative portfolio might yield, that $1 million drops to just $380,000. That's quite a difference.[17]

While hypothetical and not indicative of any particular investment (major compliance points on that disclosure!), these results spotlight the power of long-term compounding and the accelerated growth in value that occurs when the earnings generated by an investment are reinvested and thus produce even more earnings. Time is obviously critical to this process. The longer an investment can compound, the bigger it will grow as it feeds on earnings.

Ideally, each person should start investing for retirement on their first day on the job. Investor 1 had the right idea all along. But regardless of when you start saving, there's still time to harness the power of compounding. Time is on your side if you start today.

---

17 Maurie Backman, "Here's What the Wealthiest Americans Have Saved for Retirement. Good news: It's a Figure You Can Get to as Well," The Motley Fool, April 8, 2018, https://www.fool.com/retirement/2018/04/09/heres-what-the-wealthiest-americans-have-saved-for.aspx.

CASE STUDY: DAVID'S SOLUTION

Here's another example involving two hypothetical clients. Let's pretend they're a thirty-five-year-old married couple who bought a $600,000 house in Nashville. They put 25 percent down, or $150,000, so they owe $450,000, and got a mortgage at 3.5 percent interest. Their combined income is $200,000 per year, and they're putting 10 percent of their income into the husband's 401(k). The wife is self-employed and doesn't have a retirement account yet. They have $20,000 in their emergency fund but haven't started a middle bucket yet.

They're dead set on paying off their house in five years, and although they enjoy traveling and nice things, they still live within their means and tell me they have an extra $2,500 per month they could put toward the mortgage.

Overall, they have more than enough income—totaling about one-third of the price of their home—to pay off their mortgage comfortably. They put the ideal amount down, 25 percent, which is a thumbs-up. But there are still some things I'd advise them to do differently:

1. Considering their holistic picture, spending patterns, and other benchmarks, I'd recommend that instead of putting every extra penny toward the house, they build their emergency fund up to $40,000 instead of keeping it at $20,000.

2. Instead of putting 10 percent toward retirement accounts, I'd encourage them to put 20 percent. Because the wife is self-employed, she could start a SEP IRA to help them reach that 20 percent goal. This would allow them both to put money aside for retirement, making for a balanced approach.

3. This couple is only thirty-five years old; they need some easily accessible funds, which means they should build their middle bucket so they have some liquidity. They shouldn't have all their money tied up in the house and in retirement savings.

4. I'd suggest they split their $2,500 of extra cash flow each month between extra principal on the mortgage and the middle bucket. In other words, I'd advise them to put $1,250 of that extra money toward the mortgage, and the other $1,250 into the middle bucket. As their income increases, they'll continue to build both of these accounts, paying down the house at a young age and building a balanced plan at the same time.

But, David, my mortgage rate is only 3.5 percent, and I get 10 percent in the stock market. Why pay down my mortgage at all?

If I had $1 for every time I heard that question, I could pay for that Florida beach house I've been eyeing in cash.

I'd like to think that I'm in the top echelon of advisors in my profession and really good at building portfolios and growing wealth. Let's just assume—for shameless fun, not for ego—that I think even I can average 12 percent a year. First, no advisor should, or is even allowed to, guarantee returns. Second, even if I were that good, there's still a level of risk involved in the market. My point is, it's not always about returns, it's about the feeling of knocking out that debt and not having to rely on hypothetical returns that may or may not ever happen.

It's not always about returns, it's about the feeling of knocking out that debt and not having to rely on hypothetical returns that may or may not ever happen.

THE IDEAL DOWN PAYMENT FOR A HOUSE: 25 PERCENT

I always tell clients to try to put 25 percent down on a home. Sure, 10 percent might get you a mortgage. In fact, before the 2008 crash, there used to be mortgages you could get with zero percent down. But my experience over the years shows that 25 percent is ideal, plus there are several benefits to putting this much down:

- It shows you can really afford the home.
- It makes you think twice about how much you're spending on a house.
- It gives you some padding so that if we have another 2008 type of real estate meltdown, you already have a 25 percent cushion in your house.

There's no right or wrong here, but following certain principles like this, as with every part of financial planning, is the key to winning. Establishing certain nonnegotiable principles will help you avoid falling victim to emotions, which I call the "money killers."

> **Establishing certain nonnegotiable principles will help you avoid falling victim to emotions, which I call the "money killers."**

Now, what if someone has some extra money and wants to put 50 percent down? If you have enough money saved in Buckets 1, 2, and 3, and you have a good balance between all three, then I'd say, absolutely put 50 percent down.

There are also some situations in which I'd recommend paying your house off completely. For example, if you owe only $100,000 on your home and inherit $1 million or are the beneficiary of a $500,000 death benefit from a life insurance policy when a relative dies, I'd advise paying off your mortgage—if, of course, you have plenty of money in Buckets 1, 2, and 3.

In general, avoid having a paid-off mortgage as your only focus. I don't want to see you work hard for twenty years to pay off the house only to find out you have no money saved for retirement. Balance!

CHAPTER 7

WHAT'S MY MAGIC NUMBER?

Many people are fearful of retirement and endure sleepless nights, wondering, *What's the magic number to retirement?*

Let me first say this: There's no such thing as a magic number. The better question to ask is, "How do I know if I'm on track to live the life I want, whether that means retiring completely, slowing down, or making a transition into my dream job?"

The problem is that we tend to believe in the myth of the magic number. I'd say 95 percent of the time, the magic number in our heads is based on some arbitrary number, or comparison to our friends or coworkers, or from a magazine article, not from a reputable financial planner.

I had a couple in my office who had $30 million and who were unsettled because they felt their magic number was $40 million. That's right—they explained to me that if they had $10 million more, they'd feel at ease and could live comfortably on the earnings from their money (insert eye roll here, right?). That same week, a sweet lady who'd been a client for ten years decided to retire. Her plan was to live on Social Security and a small distribution from her $200,000 IRA ($800 per month). And guess what? She was happy as a clam. I'll never forget the extreme differences between these two meetings. If one person can live happily on $200,000 and another can't find happiness with a $30 million nest egg, that's proof that there's no such thing as a magic number.

However, there are five major points I'd want you to consider when trying to make sure you have enough money to retire:

1. SAVE TEN TIMES YOUR SALARY FOR RETIREMENT.

If you want to maintain your pre-retirement lifestyle for as long as you live, you should aim to amass ten times your final salary in savings by retirement. Remember, this is just a general rule of thumb to give you a targeted amount. If you're not there yet, don't panic. Just try to sock 15 percent to 20 percent of your income each year into Bucket 3 (retirement) like we discussed in chapter 4.

Ideally, you should consider reducing your current cost of living to make it happen, while also balancing time with family and enjoying experiences. I recognize this can be a struggle when things are tight, which is why it's important to build your plan looking at all the tradeoffs, pros/cons, and of course, buckets.

You can also gauge whether you're on the right track with your investments (Buckets 2 and 3) if you're hitting these benchmarks:

- At age thirty: one time your salary
- At age forty: three times your salary
- At age fifty: six times your salary

- At age sixty: eight times your salary
- At retirement: ten times your salary

For example, if you're forty-three and making $120,000 per year, according to the above benchmark—again, this is only one way, and by no means the only way, to gauge how you're doing—having $360,000 in Buckets 2 and 3 combined would be ideal.

2. WHEN YOU RETIRE, KEEP WITHDRAWALS AT 4(ISH) PERCENT.

Ask soon-to-be retirees how much they think they can pull out of their retirement plans each year and the numbers are double or sometimes triple the right amount. That's a recipe for running out of money, fast. Around 4-ish percent is safe—"ish" because when markets are down, you'll want to withdraw a little less (3.5 percent or so), but in the years when your portfolio is doing well, you can pull out a little more (4.5 percent or so). Now, this is an area where many financial planners disagree, but it's not a wrong/right scenario. I tell clients that getting it right is an art, not an exact science. You need someone who can help you ebb and flow with the ups and downs of the market and your spending patterns and make sure you stay on the right growth/withdrawal trend line.

Typically, I've seen that pulling 3 percent or so, picking up a part-time career instead of quitting work altogether, and supplementing income with Social Security can be beneficial to maintaining your retirement fund. I like to be conservative in the early years to allow a transition into this new phase.

For example, let's say Mike and Cindy are both sixty-six and have $800,000 saved in Bucket 3 for retirement. They both decide they want to retire, so they meet with their financial advisor and learn that they'll need $100,000 per year to live the way they want. This includes travel, basic expenses, health-care, home maintenance, etc. Also, this number is net of taxes, meaning they'll need $100,000 per year after any taxes.

Together, they get $40,000 from Social Security, leaving $60,000 per year that they must cover. If they take 4 percent per year from their $800,000 retirement fund, that's $32,000, still leaving a $28,000 shortfall. Plus, assuming they're in the 20 percent tax bracket, they'll need $125,000 to net $100,000 after 20 percent in taxes. This leaves a $53,000 gap between their expenses and current income.

The solution? They can either adjust their lifestyle to spend around $70,000, annually, or come up with a combined income of $50,000, annually, to accommodate their current lifestyle. Ideally, the retire-while-you-work scenario would be for each of them to pursue a passion career where they can each make $25,000 per year, enjoy what they do, and stay engaged, healthy, and connected.

4% x $800k = $32k/yr

INCOME "NEEDS"

$100k/year (or $125k before taxes)

$32k/yr (BUCKET 3) + $40k/yr (SOCIAL SECURITY) = $72k/yr

How do we get this $53k gap filled?

Life is all about trade-offs. Want to live off more income during retirement? Work part time. Want to play golf and enjoy the beach all day? Live off fixed income (Social Security and any pensions) and use no more than 4 percent or so of your retirement funds from Bucket 3.

3. KNOW WHAT YOU MEAN BY "RETIREMENT."

The folks at Age Wave and Merrill Lynch recently conducted a large piece of research on finances in retirement. They found that many people who say they're retired still earn an income working part-time or taking sabbaticals from their careers.[18] If this is how you envision retiring, it means your money can stay in retirement accounts longer and continue to grow, with you taking out a smaller percentage of principal each year. It doesn't have to be all or nothing! This is the essence of retiring while you work—people are finally starting to understand it, and it makes my little heart so happy.

4. COURSE CORRECT.

Age Wave also looked into what changes people made to help them dramatically reduce their cost of living now to save more for the future.[19]

A thirty-five-year-old decided to give up a pack of cigarettes a day, meaning they'd save $360,000 by age sixty-five (plus gain greater health, of course.)

A sixty-year-old couple planning to retire decided they'd each

18 "Work in Retirement: Myths and Motivations. Career Reinventions and the New Retirement Workscape," Merrill Lynch in partnership with Age Wave, 2014, https://agewave.com/wp-content/uploads/2016/07/2014-ML-AW-Work-in-Retirement_Myths-and-Motivations.pdf.

19 Ibid.

work twenty hours a week, giving them more money for retirement and enabling them to take Social Security later.

A sixty-five-year-old couple ready to retire sold their $325,000 New Jersey home and moved to South Carolina, where they bought a $115,000 home for cash. Adding the savings in property taxes and the cost of living, they save $28,000 a year in living expenses alone.

Weekly, we see ways clients can make trade-offs to open up so many retirement options they didn't even imagine, allowing the idea of retirement to be dynamic, not some static dollar amount or age. The days of working toward one set magic number and then stopping and doing nothing are slowly becoming less of the norm. This newer-age, retire-while-you-work mind-set is far more achievable, realistic, sustainable, healthy, and balanced. It works.

5. MAINTAIN AN EMERGENCY CUSHION.

Our industry used to think that you could get rid of the emergency cushion once you stopped working. The trouble is, that means you might not have enough flexibility to handle that spontaneous car bill; a large, unexpected medical expense; or sudden home repairs. Having money set aside specifically for emergencies can be a life-saver in retirement.

Of the three buckets, Bucket 1 for emergency funds is perhaps one of the most important. Because, let's face it: life happens—and cash is always king!

So there you have it. I hope these thoughts help you rest easier at night, plan for the future, and truly get closer to retiring while you work instead of chasing a magic number that doesn't exist.

CHAPTER 8

WHAT ARE SOME GOOD ALTERNATIVES TO PUTTING ALL OF MY MONEY IN THE STOCK MARKET?

Most financial planners primarily leverage the stock market to build investment portfolios, and there's nothing wrong with that—after all, it's how they (we) get paid. But it's also true that good financial planners usually recognize when a client is timid or skeptical of the stock market. By adding layers to financial plans, financial planners can help to alleviate these concerns.

Let me also say this about all the different "alternative investments" out there: If it sounds too good to be true, it probably is. Whether it's gold, cryptocurrencies, annuities, or real estate, all investment opportunities present a fair share of risks that must be considered.

But this chapter is not about Bitcoin. It's about being careful with investing in short-term trends and fads. And it's also about learning how to participate in risky opportunities, such as Bitcoin and well-known assets—like gold or real estate—if you have the appetite.

I love risk and swinging for the fences at the right time. Even more than that, I love hitting singles and doubles all day long when it comes to investing my clients' and my personal money. But please remember this saying that I learned my first year in the business:

There's no free lunch on Wall Street ...

... unless you attend a financial planner's "free" lunch. But even that isn't free because they'll eat up your time (and time is money!), harass you for a meeting, or put you in some high-fee product you don't need, making you pay back that lunch and more over time. My point is, every single financial decision has a tradeoff, usually involving risk.

There's no free lunch on Wall Street ...

Looking for a "risk-free" return? Well, there's always that 1 percent savings account at the bank. *Not going to cut it*, you say, which means you'll probably tell me the same thing I've heard for the past fifteen years: "David, I just want to grow my money each year and never see it go down, but I need much better than that 1 percent rate the bank's offering." You and me both.

Again—there's no free lunch on Wall Street, period. By the time we typically hear about some amazing "can't lose" investment opportunity, it's usually time to run.

I remember driving around Franklin, Tennessee, in 2008 and early 2009, when the market was near its bottom, and seeing people dressed in gold costumes. They were spinning dollar signs and arrows pointing to the Cash for Gold store down the block.

In times of stock market turmoil, the number of late-night infomercials prodding people to buy gold skyrockets, because gold is typically a fear-based investment. It's easy to appeal to inexperienced investors who are losing money in their retirement accounts by making them believe that gold's the "safe investment" or the next best thing to the dollar.

It's not that gold is or isn't a bad investment. But, over time, by building a solid diversified portfolio, people have historically done better than just owning gold alone.

Also, gold has had some extreme ups and drastic crashes, far too volatile for investment, in my opinion, and it's really only good if you have play money. If you've built all three of your buckets, have a great financial plan, and enjoy the sense of stability gold brings, or the feeling of owning a precious metal, by all means buy some. The key here is to view this as more of a hobby or collectible—not as part of your income stream for retiring while you work.

I've attended seminars where speakers would try and convince the audience (over a "free" dinner, of course) that gold is the thing to own when the economy melts and the dollar loses value. I remember thinking, *If the entire economy implodes, every McDonald's and Walmart closes, and the dollar is worthless, the last thing I'd want to own is a block of gold.* If it's that bad out there, you're probably better off owning bottled water, ammo, and cans of beans—unless you plan on hitting someone over the head with a bar of gold to get food or water!

Who knows, maybe I'm wrong, and that's fine. The point is to help you see things through a different lens when you evaluate these fads or trends. When you see something like cryptocurrency come out, selling for less than a penny, and then hike up to $11,000 per coin, with most people (including yours truly) not even fully understanding how it works, you should consider making these investments with your play money—not as part of your three buckets.

I've had clients ask me to buy them Bitcoin, for example. And we can't help them because it doesn't (at least currently) trade on a registered exchange, and it's not regulated. This type of investment violates one of my principles of building a financial plan, which is that anything we buy in your portfolio must be publicly traded, regulated, and able to sell at the click of a button. I've advised clients that if they have the appetite to play the game then, by all means, I'm their biggest cheerleader. I'll go through their three buckets to advise them on how much they can afford to lose if things go sour and make sure they never have to worry about tacking on more years before they can retire.

Here's the last point I want to make on this topic: if you speculate on a trendy investment, be sure to pull out your initial investment once you hit your target profit. For example, say you decide to put $10,000 in some trendy industry that's making headlines and billions of dollars in profits. Before you pull the trigger, speak with your advisor and ask them to hold you accountable. Say you're lucky enough to double your money, make sure they hold you to pulling out your initial $10,000 and then maybe have you put it into your three buckets. Then, if you still want to stay in the game, at least you're playing with "house money." Later, if that money crashes and burns, at least you can take comfort in knowing you didn't lose your principal. On the other hand, if that money explodes to $500,000, great—you've hit a homerun and can use it to kick start that dream business, travel more, help a friend or family member in need, or create other bucket list experiences.

I tell my clients to never own more than 5 percent of their portfolio in any one stock or investment theme. And yes, trying to get someone who has 80 percent of their Bucket 3, 401(k) money in their company stock to rethink that distribution can be the hardest fight to win for a financial planner! But there's a reason behind these philosophies—to help you manage risk and keep you on the path to retiring while you work.

SHOULD I BUY INVESTMENT PROPERTIES FOR PASSIVE INCOME?

Of all the non-stock-market investments out there, I love this strategy—*if* you can afford it and only *after* you've built the foundation in your three buckets. Buying investment real estate fits into Bucket 2, typically. (There are ways to own real estate inside your IRAs in Bucket 3, but that's a whole different set of considerations we can discuss another day.)

The idea of passive income, or mailbox money, is powerful. We work with a lot of songwriters who are fortunate enough to get these kinds of checks from their songs being played on the radio or streamed on mobile devices. Also, many of our clients have a diversified section in Bucket 2 for several rental homes, which provide them a positive net cash flow and help them pay down mortgages on these properties. Passive income gives us the luxury to dabble in other areas, have side projects and passions, and, best of all, retire while we work.

> **Passive income gives us the luxury to dabble in other areas, have side projects and passions, and, best of all, retire while we work.**

Assuming you have three to six months' worth of emergency funds in Bucket 1, I'd suggest you save enough in this bucket for a 25 percent down payment on the property you have your eyes on. Before doing this, I'd also advise having an amount at least equal to the amount of real estate you plan on purchasing available in your Bucket 2 portfolio. Meaning, if you're looking to buy a $250,000 rental house and put $62,500 (25 percent) down, it'd be ideal to have close to $250,000 in your Bucket 2 investment account. That way, you have a nice balance between liquid (your investment stock market portfolio) and non-liquid (real estate) assets. It's integral to have that portfolio in case there's a situation where you need to get rid of a property, do a major repair, or spend an extended period trying to find a tenant.

While the exact balance of real estate to cash to an investment portfolio in the stock market is subjective, these are benchmarks that have worked in the past for hundreds of clients I've seen in the last fifteen years. Start with the foundation of a good financial plan and healthy balance sheet by building your three buckets before you venture into passive income, such as real estate.

It's also absolutely fine to not want to complicate life by managing properties. Headaches, unexpected repairs, periods of vacancy, and bad renters are inevitable. But you can still earn passive income from rentals by sacrificing some of your profits and hiring a good property manager so you're not bothered with the stress of tenants and repairs. There are pros and cons to each approach, and, like anything else in life, these are simply tradeoffs you can make depending on how you want to spend your time and live your best retire-while-you-work life.

CHAPTER 9

HOW DO WE AVOID ANOTHER MARKET CRASH LIKE THE ONE IN 2008?

We don't. We strategize *around* it and plan *for* it.

We'll see another large market drop—it's just a matter of time. They often call events like the financial crisis of 2008-2009 a *black swan event*, meaning one that happens only once every hundred years or so (even though I can think of several similar to the Great Depression that happened within that time frame). But I can tell you it's likely not going to be another hundred years before we witness the next sizeable recession or even market chaos. Many of us, I know, are still hungover from 2008. And that's okay. But that's no reason to panic or live in constant anxiety based on what's scrolling across the bottom of your TV screen. That's no way to live, and certainly not how you'll enjoy the freedom of retiring while you work.

One of the many reasons I wholeheartedly believe in our three-bucket principle is because it systematically plans for these inevitable events. Below is an example to help illustrate my point.

YOUR FINANCIAL PLAN (PRE-MARKET CRASH)

Let's say you have $50,000 in your Bucket 1 emergency fund, representing three to six months of income. You feel a decent level of job stability and typically get around a $20,000 to $30,000 bonus each April, depending on the company's profits. You've been saving 20 percent of your income between the company's 401(k) and an IRA (Bucket 3). Your 401(k) has around $330,000 and your IRA has $42,000.

In this case, I'd encourage you to systematically invest $3,000 per month (assuming you can afford that after basic living expenses) into a nonretirement investment account, along with half of your annual bonuses. (I'd also suggest you travel and experience bucket list items with the other half, for balance—true to retire-while-you-work philosophy). After several years, the balance in this Bucket 2 account could be around $230,000.

> **Although no amount of planning or diversification can protect against loss, a well-thought-out plan can help provide greater stability against the next inevitable market downturn.**

Let's say you picked up a rental property two years ago, paid $275,000, and put 25 percent down from your Bucket 2 investment account. Then, the strategy above of adding money to your Bucket 2 would allow you to have equity padded in the property in case of another 2008 real estate market drop but also let you hold a solid balance in the Bucket 2 account while you generate extra cash flow through rent.

Although no amount of planning or diversification can protect against loss, a well-thought-out plan can help provide greater stability against the next inevitable market downturn.

HERE'S AN EXAMPLE:

Major stock market indices fall 40 percent over a three-month period. Your company starts laying people off after six months of this chaos, fearing a long-term recession with a huge hit to its bottom line. Bonuses are suspended.

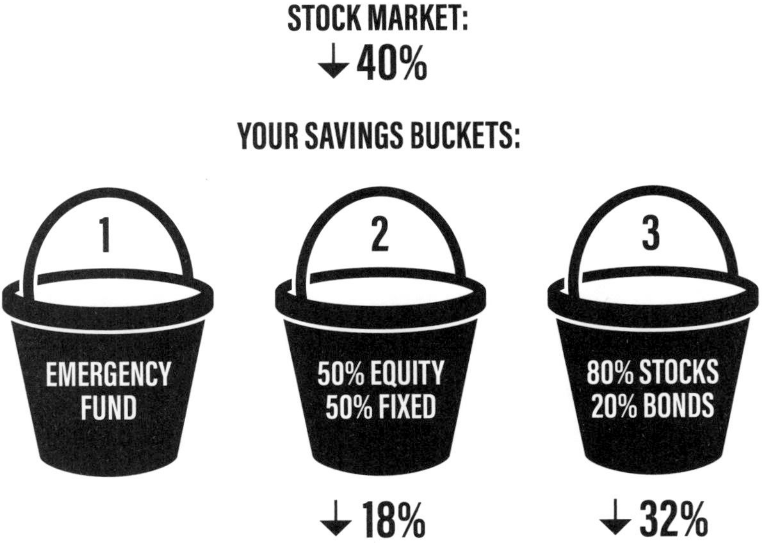

Your retirement accounts (Bucket 3) are down 32 percent on your most recent statement—a decent amount less than the broad market indices—because you're fully diversified and have a 20 percent cushion in fixed income inside these accounts. Given the specifics above, I would've suggested building your Bucket 3 with 80 percent equities (stocks) and 20 percent fixed income (bonds), or what we call a level eight.

Your Bucket 2 investment account falls 18 percent, much lower than the overall market, because we invested this as a level five with 50 percent equity and 50 percent fixed. We invested conservatively on purpose, knowing we may need to access this account at some point before ever touching your retirement accounts, and you still have the $50,000 emergency fund in Bucket 1.

This example helps show how your foundation and diversified investment plan makes it less scary to ride out wild market fluctuations.

CHAPTER 10

HOW MUCH MONEY DOES IT TAKE TO BE HAPPY?

Can money buy happiness? How much does it take to be happy? Does the pursuit of money ever stop? I've been asked these questions by some of my closest clients during deep conversations we've shared.

Can you guess how much money the happiest families make? In a recent study about how happiness and money may coincide, researchers found that those individuals making between $50,000 and $75,000 appeared to be happiest.[20] This suggests that making over $75,000 per year won't significantly improve your day-to-day happiness. Also, after a certain point, there's a diminishing level of happiness for every jump in income.

Fellow financial advisor Wes Moss in his book, *You Can Retire Sooner Than You Think*, cited $500,000 of net worth as another metric

20 LearnVest, "The Salary That Will Make You Happy (Hint: It's Less Than $75,000)," *Forbes*, April 24, 2012, https://www.forbes.com/sites/learnvest/2012/04/24/the-salary-that-will-make-you-happy-hint-its-less-than-75000/#148cb3a93247.

to examine.[21]

Of course, every family's needs and wants differ, and factors can change dependent on how much debt an individual or family has, the number of children, etc. But the average family agreed that its emotional well-being or day-to-day experiences were not affected by not having millions in the bank. To me, this was intriguing, because we're a society that constantly wants more. But I hope we're all learning together that when you chase more, it's a chase that never ends—and one that leaves you feeling lonely.

Ever heard the saying, "More money, more problems"? Above a certain income level, people start to just accumulate stuff, and then, over time, they become slaves to that stuff, trying to maintain and keep up with it, which can lead to more stress! Think about it—if you buy a third car, or a second home, the next thing you know, you'll have to do three sets of oil changes and tire rotations, and you'll have to keep up with two lawns and properties to maintain, etc., etc.

Part of the retire-while-you-work philosophy is finding ways to get into a healthier mind-set regarding your money. As a society, we have so many unhealthy attachments to money. Many people spend their lives thinking, "If only I had $1 million, I'd be happy," or, "If I made $100,000 a year, I'd be happy." Then, oftentimes, those who have $1 million start thinking they need $1.5 million to be comfortable, and so on. It never ends, and the carrot chase continues at every level. In all my years of financial advising, I can validate this with much conviction—money does *not* buy happiness.

My hope is that, together, we can start a movement to retire while we work and let the old ideal of retirement fade away. We need to realize that we're living longer and we have more resources to stay

---

21 Wes Moss, *You Can Retire Sooner Than You Think*, (New York City: McGraw-Hill Education, 2014).

healthy, if we choose. Finding passion in your job and personal life can fuel you, keep you motivated, and lessen the desire to have millions saved up for retirement.

If you've ever listened to my radio show or podcasts, you've probably heard me explain the drastic differences we've seen in our clients, ranging from the happily retired person with a $200,000 IRA to the $30 million net worth couple who thought they needed $40 million to retire happily. It's all about the mind-set and perspective—we must pursue a healthy outlook about money.

We can always have more money, but we can't buy more time! Experiences are the true legacy we leave behind. Spend your *time* with those you love, doing the things you love.

EXPERIENCES ARE WORTH MORE THAN MATERIAL THINGS.

I don't believe money alone can buy happiness. However, what if we readjusted our thinking to see that money can, in fact, allow us the chance to have experiences we may otherwise miss out on, *leading* to greater happiness?

I often think about how important it is to our overall happiness to spend money on experiences versus material things. I've learned over the years from my experience with clients and from just talking to health professionals that practicing gratitude can improve overall health, boost our mood, and help lower stress. Most inspirationally, it can help promote behaviors of generosity toward others.

Furthermore, the article went on to state that experience-based purchases were proven to elicit greater gratitude because they don't trigger social comparisons the way possessions do. Think about it. You buy a new car, but then someone else buys a luxury car, and it kills your mojo. Experiences foster an appreciation of your circumstances rather than elicit feelings of falling short or needing to measure up to others.

No, I'm not saying go crazy spending and blowing all your money on travel. But if you want to live better and feel more fulfilled, having a more experience-focused mind-set is a way to help do that!

CHAPTER 11

HOW SHOULD I BUILD A BUDGET AND MANAGE MY DEBT?

Let me start by tackling the budgeting part first. I've used the concept of a reverse budget with my clients for years, at least as a conversation starter. Many people get overwhelmed at the idea of tracking every single expense daily, following software apps on their phones, or building spreadsheets. And, yes, while it'd be ideal for everyone to live on a proactive, itemized budget, I've learned to adapt to human behavior by finding ways to help clients reach their end goal, which is to not spend all their money and neglect their financial plan.

My reverse budget philosophy makes this possible and simple—pay yourself first at the beginning of the month. Then, even if you spend away, go nuts, and run the account dry, at least you didn't neglect your three buckets. When clients tell me, "Hey, David, we'll just mail you checks for our three buckets at the end of each quarter after we see all of our expenses," I know the likelihood of that check being placed on my desk is slim. Not because of lack of intent or desire by the client, but because it's human nature to spend what we have easy access to.

I encourage you to set up automatic payments to each of your three buckets so your money goes exactly where it needs each time you get paid. This way, you've paid yourself first—and that's the most important payment!

AND NOW FOR MANAGING DEBT

There's good debt, and there's bad debt. And there are good ways and bad ways to manage both debts.

Let's start with good debt. I believe that having a mortgage on your home, or on any investment property, falls in this category—as long as you've put at least 25 percent down, ideally. These assets generally appreciate over time. So as long as you can afford the monthly payments and have a healthy down payment and equity in the property, I'm all for it.

In fact, if a client is building their three buckets and Bucket 2 has a nice-sized liquid investment portfolio, I'd advise them to consider maybe one or two investment properties—as long as they have the time to deal with it themselves or the resources to pay someone else to. Real estate is a nice diversifier of your assets but usually involves taking on some debt.

Now, if you have a massive amount in Buckets 1 and 2 and way more than you ever plan to need, you should consider paying cash and being debt free. The grass always feels better on your feet when it's paid off.

Now for bad debt. Credit cards, car loans, and boat loans equal bad debt, in my opinion. There's no judgment or shame here, so please don't read it that way. My only goal is to help you realize the types of debts you should focus on paying off versus the type that may be okay to hold on to for a longer term. When possible, I advise clients to buy a car for only what they can afford in cash out of Bucket 1, simply because a car is one of the worst investments there is, while also being a necessity. Ideally, we try and buy something a few years old where we can get 50 percent or more off the new sticker price. And I absolutely love boats, but I've yet to meet anyone with a boat who didn't say their best day with it was the day they bought it followed closely by the day they sold it (unless they were retired and using it all the time). And boats, like cars, can lose as much as 50 percent of their value in just two to three years.

Credit cards have always scared me because of the interest they can carry when they're not paid in full. As I mentioned earlier, I followed and taught some of Dave Ramsey's advice early in my career, and it was ingrained in me that credit card debt was the devil. Paying double digit interest rates for years and years can make it challenging to ever get ahead, and that's why it's so important to have that emergency fund in Bucket 1, so that once you get out of credit card debt, you never go back.

What about student loans? Great question. Student loans are kind of like an extension of good debt, in my opinion, because they're used toward an asset that, hopefully, appreciates—your knowledge. That being said, many times the rates on student loans can be fairly high or fluctuate, so I usually have my clients aggressively pay these down. We usually start with the bad debts first, paying them off completely in order of highest interest rates to lowest, while also chopping significant chunks off student loan debt.

Parents must endeavor to educate adolescent kids about the

impact of credit card debt, in essence teaching them not to spend money they don't have. A college student who's used to a certain standard of living may have a rough time adjusting to being financially independent. For instance, a pizza they buy for $20 today can end up costing them $80 because of high interest rates charges for failing to pay their credit card balance in full. Multiply that cost by every night of their college career, and it's easy to see how students can rack up thousands of dollars of debt—and work years to pay it off.

Debt happens. But instead of living in shame about past mistakes, move toward a life of retiring while you work, where you aren't a slave to a lender, but instead are in control and free to create experiences and memories.

CHAPTER 12

HOW DO I MAKE SURE MY FAMILY IS TAKEN CARE OF IF SOMETHING HAPPENS TO ME?

Last year, I realized that many of our clients—and people in general—don't have an organized plan to help surviving loved ones carry on with their finances once they're no longer around. My team has witnessed spouses grow distressed and overwhelmed by mounting bills, having no clue where important documents and assets like money, insurance policies, and estate documents are located.

Preparing your family for life events can feel like a project that's tough to tackle—you may not even know where to begin! In our office, we call these types of preparations a fire drill, because you're preparing and equipping your family for dire circumstances. A good financial advisor will be passionate about helping people plan for the what-ifs in life and offer confidence to their loved ones when the inevitable strikes.

We're all busy, so the idea of taking a Saturday to pull information together for your inevitable death (morbid, I know) is anything but fun. However, it can be very helpful for your successors.

I remember a client whose Comcast service was shut down after she lost her husband because the bill wasn't paid. She had no idea if the payments were scheduled on auto pay or if she needed to write a check. This seemingly minor setback brought her to deep tears, giving rise to the fear that she wouldn't be okay without him. It broke my heart.

> **The goal is to help your family be proactive, which can make navigating an unforeseen situation much easier for them.**

The goal is to help your family be proactive, which can make navigating an unforeseen situation much easier for them.

Part of the retire-while-you-work philosophy is to build a team of individuals around you who can handle the financials, allowing your family and loved ones to focus on important things—such as mourning, spending time with each other, praying, etc.—instead of having to worry about paying bills.

Even one piece of paper with some guidance is better than nothing. In fact, it'll probably be 90 percent of all you need.

Putting together some information shouldn't take more than a few hours. Below are some simple things that can make a huge difference.

1. WRITE DOWN ALL YOUR MONTHLY BILLS.

Next to the name of the bill, write down how it's paid (check, auto pay, etc.). Also write down where the bill payment hub is located, providing usernames and passwords to your billing accounts. Write these instructions as though you're giving them to a person who knows nothing about your home or bill payment system.

2. DO THE SAME FOR YOUR INVESTMENT ACCOUNTS.

Write, for example, "John has an IRA at *XYZ* brokerage firm with around $100,000 in it. Susie has a trust account at *XYZ* with $500,000 in it." Also, be sure to include pertinent details such as 1-800 customer service numbers as well as account numbers. You could even provide full statements—the more the better. But even a little something is better than nothing.

3. LOCATE YOUR ESTATE PLANNING DOCUMENTS.

These documents include wills, trusts, powers of attorney, living wills, etc. Give a copy to your loved ones, financial planner, and estate attorney, and keep the original in a safe place at home.

4. ORGANIZE YOUR LIFE INSURANCE POLICIES.

For example, write "$100,000 term policy on John for twenty years, bought from John Doe at *XYZ* insurance company around 2011, expires 2031. Policy should be in the closet safe. The safe code is 1234." Again, anything that helps give a starting point for your family.

Many life insurance policies go unclaimed every year!

I'm often asked, "How much life insurance do I need for my family?" I've heard many different formulas, ranging from an insurance salesperson telling one of our clients they need ten to even twenty times their income to others saying you need only as much insurance as you have debt. I don't like generic formulas, so I try to keep it simple. The purpose of life insurance is to leave your spouse and children with as clean of a financial slate as possible should you pass away.

Calculate all of your debts (credit cards, car loans, student loan, mortgages, etc.), think about how much your kids would need for college, and, finally, add the amount of income replacement your spouse would need to keep the household running without you. If your spouse doesn't work and relies on solely your income, I'd have at least five years of income (plus, enough to pay off all debts and college) so that your spouse has enough time to go back to school or enter the workforce and build up a sufficient earning stream. Don't just blindly buy a bunch of life insurance without going through an exercise like this to see what's best for your family. Insurance isn't about getting rich; it's about protecting your family and making sure they're not left in a financial mess.

5. LIST YOUR BANK ACCOUNTS.

For example, "We have two checking accounts, two savings accounts, a Christmas account, and a travel account." Write down where they're located, approximate balance, etc. People sometimes forget about certain accounts for several years because they might receive a different statement for it or because the statement goes to an old address.

Funny story: Every six months, one of my funniest clients would call me befuddled and say, "David, I think I found a $50,000 CD I didn't even know we had!" I'd laugh and say, "Must be nice to have that problem." But imagine if, God forbid, he'd passed without ever discovering these accounts and his family ended up in need of funds for a medical bill, a debt that was stunting their livelihood, or some other emergency—how crazy and unfortunate would that have been? That's why it's important to keep track of your accounts—and write them down.

6. OTHER THINGS TO INCLUDE

Passwords, logins, social media information (to remove accounts), email access information, etc. are good information to include. When you're jotting down this private information, be smart about where you store it. Last year, the FBI was on our radio show, and they suggested having it written down and stored in a safe or maybe placed as a bookmark in a book that sits on a shelf. Some people save this information on their computers and lock the file, but that can be problematic if the person who needs access to it isn't able to open it. Alternatively, if you have a trusted financial planner who you can leave instructions with, tell your family to contact that person if something happens to you. Don't obsess, just be smart—there's no perfect plan.

The goal is to enjoy life, to be a good steward of your resources, and to help others—not to stress and detract from your happiness.

Many people don't like to think about unplanned life events that can be sad or depressing, but the reality is, life happens. And with a bit of preparation, everyone can feel a little more secure when it does. You can create this prep plan in two hours, this week. I'm serious; I believe in you!

Remember, there's comfort in knowing that in case something unplanned happens, you have a plan! The more comfort you can bring through planning, the better you can enjoy your journey.

CHAPTER 13

SHOULD I INVEST ONLINE MYSELF OR USE A FINANCIAL ADVISOR?

People often ask, "How should I invest? Should I do it online to save on fees, or should I hire a financial planner?" In most cases, especially when there may be substantial assets involved, financial advisors are the best option because, as you'll see in this chapter, we get to know you, your concerns, needs, and dreams, and we provide personalized advice that takes those important factors into account. For beginning investors, robo-advisors (apps and software programs you access online) are sometimes the best option.

> Everything has a cost, and fees are an issue only in the absence of value.

This isn't a shameless plug, but I've been blessed to have a group of loyal clients who've been through the ups and downs of the market and who really understand our value as financial advisors. What I've learned is this: everything has a cost, and fees are an issue only in the absence of value.

Sure, you can do your own financial planning for free, but do you want that burden or stress? As humans, we're not wired to operate alone. We're made to collaborate with others and share accountability. This is true in all aspects of life in my opinion; I've learned this lesson from several mentors and coaches I've had throughout the years.

As in any profession, some financial advisors add value tenfold, and others are a total rip-off. As an example, let's pick on attorneys. If you've ever had to deal with a complicated legal situation, having an attorney who cares, bills you fairly, listens to you, and helps you get your desired compensation is worth every penny, even if their fee is $500 an hour. If you try to save money by hiring the attorney whose fee is $200 an hour, but he bills you for twice as many hours, forgets the details of your case, and ends up getting you a lackluster result, you haven't saved money at all.

Sure, on the front end it might seem like you saved a couple hundred bucks an hour, but on the backend you ended up netting more loss than you can probably calculate. That's hard for a lot of people to see initially because they're focused on the *cost* rather than the *value*. I can attest to this. When I was faced with a legal situation, I hired an attorney who charged a high hourly rate, but he earned all his money in the beginning by pursuing the right path in our lawsuit against a former employer.

Each month I opened his bill, I felt like throwing up because he cost so much. But we were thrilled with the end result. I learned a lot through that process about where it makes sense to cut corners and where it doesn't. Like attorneys, financial planners and good doctors are not people to hunt bargains on. Heart surgery might cost $100,000, but I don't ever see anybody trying to find the cheapest heart surgeon. This is the definition of being pennywise and pound foolish.

MY CONFESSION

I'll humble myself by telling you the story about how I tried to save money buying a house. It was a monumental disaster.

I tried to buy a house without a real estate agent, and oh, boy—shame on me! I know several friends and clients who do real estate for a living. Did I consult with them? No. To save on the six percent commission, I went the do-it-yourself route, even though I'd never done that before. For all my previous properties, I'd always worked with agents, so I knew better.

There was this one property I fell in love with. The location was perfect and the home even had a unique architectural design. I didn't want it to get sold out from under me, so I bought it on the spot, without an inspection.

Since then, I've paid for that mistake tenfold. I could have funded the Taj Mahal for the amount I spent on getting this place ready for resale. The HVAC had issues I'm still working on, the sewer pump was defective, and the latches on some very expensive German windows were broken. The home came with beautiful high-end appliances, but even they had issues, such as a broken ice maker in the freezer and burning coils on the oven. Even some of the wiring on the lighting was bad, warranting a visit from an electrician. Put simply, the investment was a money pit.

Also, because I didn't have an agent representing me, I ended up paying for things a seller typically pays for—as a buyer, the contract wasn't worded in my favor. I played into my emotions and overpaid for the property. Had I worked with an agent, who would have probably helped me think logically, I could have paid $100,000 less than I did.

As long as I'm making fun of myself, let me tell you another true, relevant story. One time (at a different property), instead of hiring a handyman, I decided to change a faulty kitchen light on my own. I turned off the breaker and then went to work, poking around in the ceiling. While up there, I felt a sudden zing course through me—I'd shocked myself! It turns out, I'd turned off the wrong breaker! But that's not all. When I got shocked, I jerked, throwing my screwdriver through the drywall on the other side of the kitchen. At the end, not only did I end up having to get an electrician, but I also ended up having to hire someone to put up drywall and do a paint job over the damaged wall. If I'd simply paid someone $200 at the beginning to take care of the light, I would have saved myself a lot of headache—and money. True story.

> That mistake helped me learn another valuable lesson: hire someone for everything that's not your personal strong suit.

That mistake helped me learn another valuable lesson: hire someone for everything that's not your personal strong suit.

This holds true at our firm, too. I no longer pay the bills or keep the accounting books, even though I'm a CPA. It was hard for me to let go of that control. But now I have a CFO whom I trust to do all that for me, thanks to the lessons I've learned.

MISTAKES ARE LEARNING OPPORTUNITIES.

Maybe you've heard the ancient story about the cobbler whose children had no shoes. Or about the doctor whose kids were sick. My situation is similar. I can be the best financial planner for other clients and help them distance their emotions from important financial decisions. But when it comes to making my own decisions, it's not that easy. That's why I now consult with another group of financial planners whenever I'm getting ready to make a big personal decision—and they do the same with me. We keep each other in check because we realize that emotions are, again, money killers. And even professionals get caught up in them. So I understand how my clients feel. My job is to make sure you don't make bad decisions based on emotions.

Getting back to my examples, would I have preferred to avoid those ridiculous decisions? Of course. But I'm turning them into positive learning experiences, and I'm very thankful that I had my three buckets so these mistakes didn't disrupt my financial plan. Buckets 1 and 2 saved me; I was able to pay for the repairs, and I can take some funds out of Bucket 2 if I end up losing money on the house. I'm still right on track.

TRYING TO TIME THE MARKET IS A LOSING GAME.

One of the biggest and most costly mistakes investors make is pulling their money out of the stock market when there's a downturn. This is an emotional, knee-jerk reaction. One of the most valuable services we offer clients is to be the voice of reason during times like that.

Studies show that most people who yank their money out of the stock market at the worst of times end up buying back when the market is soaring high. Alternatively, they would have been better off (financially and blood-pressure wise) if they'd just stayed put and avoided rash decisions. You have better odds in Vegas than you do attempting to read the mind of the stock market.

Trying to time the market is a losing game; the odds are immensely against you. During the 2008 crisis, we had only two clients pull their money out against our advice, and they're still not back in the market today. They've put all their money in the bank, even making as low as one percent off their funds. Not only that, but they've grown to resent the stock market so much that they can't justify getting back in today at what they believe to be high prices. It's become a terrible mind game for them, a mental block.

In August 2011, Fidelity Investments studied the way 401(k) plan participants handled their accounts during the 2008-2009 market crisis. Here's what they found:[22]

- Plan participants who dropped their equity allocation to zero between October 1, 2008, and March 31, 2009, and kept it there, experienced an average 2 percent increase in their 401(k) account balances through June 30, 2011.
- Investors who changed their equity allocation to zero but returned to some level of equity investment after the downturn showed an average increase of 25 percent in their account balances.
- The clear winners were the investors who maintained their allocation to stocks during that same period. By mid-2011, they had average account balance increases of 50 percent. And the 401(k) participants who continued contributing *during* the downturn experienced average account increases of 64 percent, compared to average account increases of 26 percent for investors who stopped contributing completely!

This is one of the many reasons why we all need professional help. Playing the emotional roller coaster of the stock market is a losing proposition, period.

22 Steve Vernon, "Study: 401(k) Investors Who Stayed the Course in 2008–09 Were Big Winners," CBS MoneyWatch, August 18, 2011, https://www.cbsnews.com/news/study-401k-investors-who-stayed-the-course-in-2008-09-were-big-winners/.

When there's a market storm, hunker down in your proverbial storm cellar, and ride it out. Don't make sudden moves. Learn from the many who've panicked, reacted on emotion, and lost fortunes.

Playing the emotional roller coaster of the stock market is a losing proposition, period.

Don't play the game. Build your buckets, know their places in your plan, let those buckets do their jobs, and hire professional help.

THE VALUE OF AN ADVISOR

About ten years ago, I remember attending a workshop by a well-known advisor named Nick Murray. He wrote a book called *Simple Wealth, Inevitable Wealth*, in which he talks about the value of an advisor. Something he said in it has stuck with me through the years: Say you pay an advisor 1 percent a year for maybe 10 years while the market is going up. At some point, you start thinking, *Gosh, I could have saved 10 percent over the previous 10 years because everything's been going up. Why do I need to pay an advisor for advice?*

The simple answer is this: A good advisor earns when times get bad. It's easy to make money when the economy and the market are booming. It's a million times harder to navigate the turbulence and stay in the game during the chaos.

Let's look at an example. Say you really can earn the same year-over-year return as your advisor. You feel like this is your gift and your passion, and you really enjoy spending time handling your investments. That's great. More power to you. There are many people out there who could arguably get the same performance on a portfolio as advisors like me. But then, let's say, that another 2008-like year happens, and you get worried because the market is falling 10, 20, or 30 percent. Fear gets hold of you, and you end up cashing out while you're down 40 percent, convinced that the media are right, and the market's going to fall 50, 60, or 70 percent. You just want to stop the bleeding. The losses you incur by pulling out of the market will be much worse than if you weathered the storm. Trust me on this.

I've had so many clients who, without us behind them, would have yanked their money out when the market was at the bottom. But let's say you guessed right—you pull out, and the market keeps falling a bit further. Then it starts to bounce back. But every time it seems like it's rebounding, it drops again. Soon, you get busy at work, and tell yourself that once it stabilizes, you're going to get back in at the bottom and time it right. The next thing you know, it's jumped above where you cashed out, and it's still bouncing around so much that you can't keep up. Finally, you end up buying back in. Please don't do this!

Early in my career, I was trained that our value as advisors was picking the right investments and focusing on returns, returns, returns. It's all about returns. When I was in my mid-twenties, I asked some of the top financial advisors in the United States if they'd mentor me. I became a sponge, soaking in everything I learned. As I worked with these top five to ten experts, I asked each one of them some of the same basic questions, such as, *What would you say your real value to your clients has been over the past forty years? What do you charge, and do your clients feel your cost is fair?*

The answers I got from each of them were near identical. The advisors almost unanimously said that the real value of an advisor lies in their ability to help clients build a financial plan, make progress toward long-term goals, stay accountable to the plan, and keep emotions isolated from decision-making. And every one of them said their clients rarely questioned their fees, other than at the beginning, or during the first down market, when they'd ask, "Am I really paying you a fee while I'm losing money?" But once they got to the other side of the bear market, they understood, and they never questioned the advisors again.

I've now been in the business long enough where I can confirm similar experiences with clients who faced the down markets of 2001 and 2008.

Regarding my question about what the advisors charged, I was told, "That's the wrong question. The right question is what *value* do we provide?" (And we wonder why the financial industry gets picked on for lack of transparency … eye roll.)

ABOUT FINANCIAL ADVISORS' FEES

Speaking of fees, what's the average fee financial advisors charge? It varies, of course. I've seen fees as high as 2 percent of the investor's total assets. I think that's too high for investors with millions of dollars in assets, but it is arguably reasonable for smaller accounts, those under $250,000. The typical industry average for fees is 1.5 percent on accounts that contain up to $1 million (some advisors charge 1.25 percent) and an average of 1 percent for accounts that contain $1 million and more. You might see fees below 1 percent and negotiable fees for accounts above the $5 million range, but basically, 1 percent is a good rule of thumb. The fee will be a little more if you have less than $1 million and a little less as the numbers get bigger.

The best advice I can give you is to find an advisor who coaches you, who doesn't talk over your head, who listens to you, who has the heart of a teacher, and who has the right credentials. Now, I'm a little biased here because I'm a CERTIFIED FINANCIAL PLANNER™

The best advice I can give you is to find an advisor who coaches you, who doesn't talk over your head, who listens to you, who has the heart of a teacher, and who has the right credentials.

(CFP®) professional, and a certified public accountant (CPA). But I strongly feel that both designations are needed and desirable for an advisor to understand the complex tax side of this business, as well as the financial side.

People who've earned the CFP® certification have been trained rigorously in six different areas: estate planning, tax planning, investment planning, ethics, insurance planning, and retirement planning. I recommend working with an advisor who has that certification. Also, when you're looking for a financial advisor, be wary of those trying to sell you products. Professional financial planners are fee-based. They're there to help you build a financial plan; the products are just a means to the end, which is why products should be the last thing they discuss with you, probably around the third meeting or so. A financial advisor should not lead with their products; otherwise, they're just glorified salespeople representing a firm and selling the product of the week to get a bigger commission or win an incentive trip.

Look for a fee-based financial advisor who charges a percentage of your assets with no contract, no upfront commissions, no back-end commissions, and no surrender penalties for taking out your money. Your financial advisor should put you on the same side of the table that they're on. Everybody has a common goal, and that's to grow your money over time. If the market is up and your accounts are growing, the fees will be a bit higher. During bad times, like 2008, where the market is tanking, financial advisors bust their tails to lose less than the market because their income goes down every bit as much as yours—they feel the pinch just like you do.

WHAT ABOUT ROBO-ADVISORS?

Today, we hear a lot of talk about robo-advisors. These are software apps or computer programs that run algorithms to determine what your best potential investments might be. For a while, we were seeing announcements for a lot of seminars that were advertised with headlines like, "Is this the death of the financial advisor?"

You can hire a robo-advisor for, let's say, half a percentage or a quarter of a percentage. Their fees are low, but you get no personalized service. You don't get the benefit of a trusted advisor—a real person, advising you to rethink a big move that you're making based off emotions.

I was on a panel at a national conference with five thousand advisors. Someone asked me, "David, are you nervous about robo-advisors taking over your business and clients?"

My response was, "No, I'm not, and here's why." Then I went on to explain that, as humans, we're wired for connection. We need a team, and we need face-to-face connection. We need people to hold our hands through the good times and the bad. A computer can't do that—at least not yet. Also, our clients have been with us for a while. They value our advice, and they recognize the worth in having someone they can call, trust, talk to, shake hands with, hug, and laugh with.

> **I believe in an abundance mentality versus a scarcity mentality.**

I believe in an abundance mentality versus a scarcity mentality. There are many people out there who need sound financial advice, and, realistically, we can work with only so many clients. So we'll choose those who value and desire human advice. Those who feel like they don't need that and can do fine with a computer can choose that option.

I'm not worried about robo-advisors. In fact, I think they're a good option for people who are just getting started and don't meet the minimum assets required by a good fee-based financial planner. I think it's better for them to use something like this, which is inexpensive, than for them to go to a financial advisor who's going to sell them a bunch of products they don't need just to make a fat commission.

I see it happen all the time. People come to us once they meet the minimum, and they're in all the wrong products. It's hard to unravel that. If they approach us before they meet the minimum, I try to do them a service by saying, "It doesn't make sense for you to pay our fee yet, so I'd rather you go and do something online." I'll help them get started. And then, when they do meet our minimum, we're happy to welcome them as clients.

When we accept new clients, we don't look just at their assets. We know that not all of our clients are going to be older folks or people who have $10 million. In fact, we want to work with younger clients, as well, who are ambitious and also with people who don't have tons of money. So we consider other factors, too, such as compatibility and coachability. Do we like this client? Is this somebody we want in our family for the next twenty or thirty years? Is this somebody we feel really wants advice and is going to listen to us, follow the plan, and stick with it? Or are they just kicking the tires, looking for someone to validate them?

If you've met or know of good advisors you want to work with long term, but you don't meet their minimum requirements, you can consider other reputable resources that have inexpensive platforms and will allow you to gain sturdy footing in the market. A good fee-based planner should point you in that direction, maybe even giving you some free input to help get you started. Then, a few years down the road when it makes economic sense, you can return to your desired advisor.

CHAPTER 14

WHEN SHOULD I TAKE SOCIAL SECURITY?

This ranks up there as one of the most commonly asked questions I get, centered around one of the most misunderstood concepts. Social Security brings with it many different scenarios and rules, but I want to hit on some high-level key points. Otherwise, I might, again, cause heads to nod or eyes to roll to the back of heads. So stick with me here.

First of all, nearly 60 percent of people take Social Security benefits early, typically at age sixty-two.[23] Why? From my experience this happens for two reasons: (1) a lack of understanding or knowledge of how it works ("I guess I'll just take it now since I qualify"), and (2) fear that it won't be there later.

The reality is, if you qualify at age sixty-two to take Social Security, but your full retirement age is sixty-six, you'll see about a 7 to

23 Peter Finch, "It's Tempting to Take Social Security at 62. You Should Wait," *New York Times*, August 31, 2018, https://www.nytimes.com/2018/08/31/business/social-security-retirement.html.

8 percent raise each year you wait. In fact, you can actually postpone taking the benefits until age seventy, at which point you'd get the largest amount possible—again, with a 7 to 8 percent raise each year. Tell me where you can get as close to a guaranteed rate of return at 7 to 8 percent anywhere. As I write this book, you're lucky if you find a one-, two-, or three-year CD at more than 2 percent.

So here's my point, and what I typically tell clients when it comes to Social Security: Unless you desperately need that check to make ends meet at age sixty-two, or if you're in really poor health, wait until your full retirement age (typically sixty-six, but that can vary according to birth year) and get the benefit of a nice raise you likely won't find anywhere else. Moreover, if you're in a position where you don't need it at sixty-six, you're still working and loving your career, and your health is good, then wait until seventy.

Unless you desperately need that check to make ends meet at age sixty-two, or if you're in really poor health, wait until your full retirement age.

It's really a game of breaking even, meaning guessing how long you'll live and planning accordingly. I jokingly tell clients, "If you can tell me how long you'll live, I can build you the perfect financial plan." They usually laugh (in-person delivery is key!). But somewhere around seventy-eight or so is the break even, meaning if you live to be eighty-five, you're likely better off waiting as long as possible for Social Security. If you pass away any time before that, you'd probably have done better turning on that income at sixty-two.

If you choose to take it early, one thing to be careful of is that your income doesn't end up lowering the benefit you receive. Basically, until you reach full retirement age, your benefit can decline $1 for every $2 you make over the current permissible limit (around $17,000 in 2018). The last thing you want to do is draw too early, forego the 7 to 8 percent raise, *and* have a reduction in benefits.

It's no secret that the federal government has promised benefits well in excess of the payroll taxes needed to pay for them. And because Social Security is something to be paid in the future, it's possible to make adjustments to it in the present. Potential options include changing the taxation of earnings, changing the benefit formula, raising the retirement age, or reducing the cost-of-living adjustments. The government could even eradicate the shortfall today by simply eliminating the taxable maximum.

While these seem like easy solutions, politicians (don't even get me started) have avoided these decisions like the plague. As politics tend to go in this country, we kick the can down the road until a big deadline or crisis hits. Either way, there are adjustments that will, in my opinion, likely be made before the government ever lets Social Security collapse.

In the meantime, get with your financial advisor and have an analysis run for you to make sure you're doing what's best for your situation. Please don't do what many people do and just take Social Security when you think you're supposed to. Our industry really isn't *that* bad, we do like to help people!

CHAPTER 15

HOW DO POLITICS IMPACT INVESTING?

Winston Churchill once said, "Americans always do the right thing but only after exhausting all other options." While hating the American government has seemingly become a favorite past time for many, it's a horrible investment strategy.

I get asked all the time whether the market does better under a republican or democratic president. The reality is that gridlock in Washington has usually worked best for the stock market—meaning, a democratic president and republican-controlled congress or vice versa. Our Founding Fathers nailed it when they came up with the principle of checks and balances, empowering our country, despite its many pitfalls and struggles, to thrive by preventing any one person or party from taking us off course. For you football fans, I like to think of it as our country fighting between opposing forty-yard lines, with checks and balances preventing us from getting too far down one end of the field or the other. Sometimes this can be frustrating, especially when it feels we can't make progress on issues like Social Security that seem to have such obvious solutions.

Investors who wait until their candidate of choice from their preferred party occupies 1600 Pennsylvania Avenue should recognize how that's worked out in the past. A $10,000 investment in the Dow Jones[24] in 1897 would have grown to $4.3 million by 2015. By contrast, if you only invested when your party was in office and then sold whenever the other party took control, that same investment would be worth $4 million less!

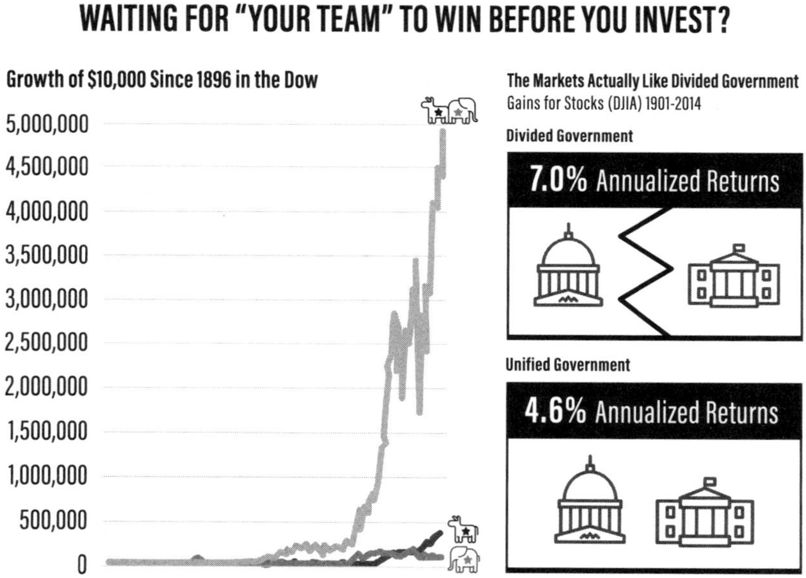

Source: *Compelling Wealth Management Conversations,* Oppenheimer Funds, 2018: 36, https://www.oppenheimerfunds.com/advisors/programs#slide_1.

Investing in the market might appear to make most sense when all political parties are being compromising and cooperative, allowing more to get accomplished. While philosophically I might agree with that logic, the truth is actually the opposite—markets tend to do best

24 The Dow Jones Industrial Average is an unmanaged index of thirty large capitalization stocks and cannot be invested into directly. Past performance is no guarantee of future success.

when there's gridlock.

But what about the country's growing deficits? I get this question all the time when I do speaking engagements—many investors are concerned about the size of these annual deficits and the growing national debt.

First, yes, typically we spend more than we bring in as a country. Our big-ticket spending items are entitlements (Social Security, Medicare, etc.) and defense spending. And our revenue comes from income and corporate taxes. We make up for the difference in spending primarily by borrowing money from ourselves but also from foreign countries like China and Japan.

Do I think this is a concern and wish we spent less than we made? Of course. If I advised clients to operate their businesses or personal households the way the government does, I would, by no means, be an admirable financial planner. But it's a bit different when you're the federal government and have money printers in your own basement.

In my opinion, our national debt and deficits aren't disappearing anytime soon. The cost of being on the sidelines and boycotting your investment philosophy because of fear, anger, or resentment to the government's fiscal policies is a losing proposition for you and your family.

The cost of being on the sidelines and boycotting your investment philosophy because of fear, anger, or resentment to the government's fiscal policies is a losing proposition for you and your family.

I do my best to not engage in politics being in my line of work, primarily because my job is to help clients stay focused and protect them from bad decisions. I will, however, step up on my soapbox and say the following: This country needs, and will thrive best off, positivity and optimism, not negativity and hate.

Even from a marketing perspective, look at arguably the two most brilliant marketing campaigns ever run in voting history—Obama's "Hope and Change" and Trump's "Make America Great Again."

In 2008, when the country was feeling scared and hopeless, Obama's message was perfectly timed, pulling the heartstrings of voters who desperately needed to hear that hope was there and change was coming. In 2016, the nation was overwhelmingly frustrated with politics in general, resentful of the system that seemed to be deteriorating the core values that made America the best country in the world. Trump's slogan fired up his voting base and enough undecided voters to help him win the election. Voters needed to hear the same "Hope and Change" message Obama had so eloquently delivered earlier, but this time in hopes of making the country great again.

Here's my hope and wish for America: I hope we can find common ground and resist both parties at the extreme ends of their beliefs; beware of the crowd at extremes. Balance and compromise is everything, especially if you want to see gradual and effective change toward keeping us strong and united.

I'm David Adams, and I'm running for President of the United States. (Kidding. Just always wanted to say that and see what it sounded like. I digress.)

PART 3

RETIRE WHILE YOU WORK—OTHER VALUABLE LIFE LESSONS

These chapters are some of my favorites. Mainly because they aren't boring financial talk but rather lessons that can help us lead much more fulfilling, interesting, and loving lives. The ability to live in this space is the cornerstone of truly retiring while you work and living your best life.

CHAPTER 16

VULNERABILITY, AUTHENTICITY, AND CONNECTION—THE TRIFECTA

The word vulnerability itself is uncomfortable. Sharing your feelings with those closest to you—yuck, right? Or even harder maybe, sharing with those you aren't close to at all. Brené Brown couldn't say it better:[25]

> *Courage starts with showing up and letting ourselves be seen … Because true belonging only happens when we present our authentic, imperfect selves to the world, our sense of belonging can never be greater than our level of self-acceptance.*

It's taken our culture a while to acknowledge this realization. Until we accept ourselves, flaws and all, how can we truly feel a sense of belonging, or find our place in the world? Think about someone

25 Brené Brown, *Daring Greatly: How the Courage to Be Vulnerable Transforms the Way We Live, Love, Parent, and Lead,* (New York City: Avery, 2015).

who retires. After their identity has been defined by their career for forty-plus years, do they accept who they are outside of their title? Are they ready to belong in a world that doesn't involve them going to an office, or talking about what they do? You've probably experienced dialogue that goes something like this:

"Hi, I'm David. What's your name?"

"Susan. Nice to meet you. What do you do, David?"

Why is that the first question people ask? Why isn't it, "What do you like to do in your free time?" Or, "Tell me about your family?" Or, "Tell me about your most exciting trip?"

That might sound farfetched that, in the not-so-distant future, robots (with the help of artificial intelligence) will take over nearly half of all human jobs. But, just for a minute, think about what it would mean. In this new reality, when someone asks you to share something about yourself, what would you say?

It's important we present ourselves, and find internal self-worth, as our authentic selves. Part of retiring while you work is knowing what you want out of life and who you are outside your career. The ideal goal is to pursue your passion so that work blends in with pleasure. Remember, in part 1, when I said you don't have to love your job to love your life. Think of your job as a means to an end—leading a life of fulfillment. And have your job serve as a fundraiser for your dreams.

You're way more than what you do to earn a living. So make sure people know you in ways you want them to see you. Are you comfortable presenting your true, authentic self to the world, versus hiding behind a title or your highlight reel on social media? I've witnessed many people build their three buckets, hit the pinnacle of financial success, and walk the retire-while-you-work path only to find themselves in a lonely place with lots of money but few deep-rooted relationships. However, if you allow yourself to be vulnerable and open up to those you want to truly connect and do life with, you'll unlock connections that will pave the road to true happiness and fulfillment. And after all, retiring while you work is about creating experiences and memories with others, not accumulating a bunch of worthless green paper.

CHAPTER 17

THE POWER OF SAYING NO

I'm a people pleaser. And although that might sound nice, sweet, selfless, and noble, it can actually be very unhealthy for all parties. It's taken me a long time (thirty-nine years and counting) to understand the challenges I create when I try to make everyone else happy at the expense of my own well-being. Every day, I work on improving, but it will be a lifelong journey. Awareness is the first step, though, so now when I realize I'm doing it, I'm cognizant about stopping and questioning myself.

People pleasers hate saying no to people because it means we're letting them down, right? No. Wrong. (See how powerful that was?!) When you over-commit and say *yes*, while knowing you are limited by time, you end up not putting your best foot forward. Over time, you dilute yourself and/or your business brand. And what you initially set out to do—please people—actually turns out to have the opposite effect, which is your biggest fear: disappointing others. Here's how it works. To please everyone, you burn the midnight oil at 50 percent and deliver subpar products or experiences. At the end, you feel tired from overworking yourself, ashamed for not giving it your all and, worse, those around you are either disappointed and/or can tell you didn't give them the focus they deserved. That can make them feel small or insignificant in your eyes. Terrible, right?

If you feel you need to say yes—for example in business—but you know you can't give it your all, then delegate. You pay people on your team or in your organization to help maintain and grow the business, so utilize them. Fight the unhealthy urge to be a control freak. "Easier said than done," says the guy who was supposed to have a writer help organize his thoughts and chapters but, instead, decided to write every single word of this book himself.

You'll deliver better quality and experience sincere connections with customers and loved ones by making your "yes" moments your best efforts.

And if you can't, or don't, feel comfortable delegating, then do the right thing for yourself and for your loved ones: say *no*. It might feel rude, harsh, unloving, or uncomfortable at first, but like anything else, over time, it'll become easier. You'll deliver better quality and experience sincere connections with customers and loved ones by making your "yes" moments your best efforts.

SIMPLICITY—THE BEST WORD EVER

Okay, maybe not *ever,* but it's been a pretty powerful word in the past few years for me, many of my clients, and our culture as a whole. Downsizing, carrying a credit card versus cash, really choosing anything that removes the complexities from our brains so we can be more present with those we love. Clearing the clutter in our brains creates space and capacity to dream again, similar to uttering that previously dreaded word, *no*.

DON'T SPREAD YOURSELF TOO THIN.

Think Post-it Notes. My mentor George asked me one time, "How many people could you call at two o'clock in the morning for help, and they wouldn't say anything except, 'Tell me where to go'?" That really made me think. He advised having a small list of names, enough to fit on a Post-it Note, of people you can count on always, no matter what. If you have three to five, consider yourself beyond blessed.

Oftentimes, we try to go an inch deep and a mile wide in life. For example, we may have hundreds of surface friends. You know, the people you check in with every few months or grab lunch with twice a year. By no means is that a bad thing, as we all get busy and life only gets busier as we get older. Connecting with as many people as you can and choose to is great. But should we also learn to say no to some of these connections? Yikes.

I've spoken to multiple clients toward the end of their journeys, asking for wisdom and advice. Often, they've told me that they wished they'd invested more into less—people, cars, houses, businesses, groups, you name it. Going a mile deep and maybe a few feet wide, now there's great wisdom in that.

Applying this to other areas of life also holds true, as in our earlier example of learning to say no so you don't overcommit and spread yourself thin. Mastering this will pay dividends during your retire-while-you-work journey.

Quality, not quantity. This year, say *yes* to less and *no* more often. You'll create more space and capacity to retire while you work.

Remember, it's two degrees at a time—small changes create small opportunities to get you closer to your goals. And several two-degree changes start building up to a full circle.

CHAPTER 18

THREE CRITICAL BUSINESS PRINCIPLES

I've messed up while growing my business—a lot. But each time, I've learned valuable lessons and emerged a slightly stronger leader and entrepreneur. Below are a few that are most important in leading you to the retire-while-you-work journey.

1. FIND YOUR "WHY."

Everything changes when you figure out your "why." "Why" inspires "wow." What does that mean? It means that when you're operating in your "why," it's nearly impossible for others to not feel your energy, authenticity, and passion, and thus experience some form of amazing moment.

If you set out to make meaning, you'll make money. If you set out solely with the goal of making money, it's unlikely you'll find meaning in your endeavors. Do you know your "why"? I mean, do you really believe in it to your core?

In his book, *Start with Why*, Simon Sinek says, "People don't buy what you do, they buy why you do it."[26] It took me years to really understand this, and for our firm's "why" to become clear. Our first ten years in business, we had mission statements and cool taglines on our website—typical stuff. But they really were just marketing materials that did what they were supposed to: look and sound good to people and check the boxes, if you will.

It took major life changes and personal upheaval in 2012 for me to understand why I show up every day. But once it's clear, boy is it clear. I realized I couldn't have made it without a team by my side—my parents, the firm's COO Chevonne, my mentor George, my men's group. And there it was, the "why":

Helping people restore vital balance and financial strength through life's many transitions.

People need people. We're wired for connection, and when we're vulnerable and at our weakest, we need a support group. It's easy to perform and make major decisions when you're at full strength, but what about when you've just lost your spouse of forty years? Or when you get fired from a job you counted on for retirement savings? I got my support when I needed it most, so I thought, why not leverage my career in some way to be that support for others?

And there it was, the "why": Helping people restore vital balance and financial strength through life's many transitions.

But the other component of our firm comprises something else I wholeheartedly believe: Doing business with people who believe

26 Simon Sinek, *Start with Why*, (New York City: Portfolio, 2009).

what you believe. For us, that means working with clients who are coachable, likeable, kind, generous, and want to experience life and retire while they work.

Once you identify your "why" for your personal life and business, you'll feel an entirely new level of confidence and passion. And passion is contagious. What's your "why"?

2. HIRE CLIENTS THE WAY YOU WOULD CHOOSE FRIENDS.

Boy, this is a tough one, and it sure took me a while to figure it out. In fact, it was just a few months ago that it all clicked for me.

In our businesses, we're often coached to analyze everything based on profits. What our account minimums are, or which client relationships aren't working well and are costing us money. Obviously, you can't run a business losing money, and you have to understand what a profitable client looks like on paper.

But what if every time you considered bringing on a new client, you looked at it the same way you do when building a new friendship with someone? Of course, if you run a business, such as a retail store where there isn't necessarily a long-term relationship with every client, this may not apply to you. But it still absolutely could apply to vendors you choose to partner with, right?

In cases where a long-term business relationship could exist, ask yourself if you really want to do life with that person. Are they worth the energy? Do they bring joy to what you do every day? Life is too short to work with people who aren't coachable, or who aren't kind to your staff, or who are just flat out negative people who kill your energy.

3. YOUR EMPLOYEES ARE YOUR BIGGEST ASSET.

If you own a small business, or any sized business, your employees are your biggest asset and are crucial to helping you walk your retire-while-you-work swagger. I've been fortunate enough to have been mentored by the best leaders in the industry, who've all stressed the importance of this philosophy.

Be generous, and live under the abundance versus scarcity mentality in your company. Without your team, after all, there's no business. So ask yourself, "What can I do to show my staff I value them?"

> **Be generous, and live under the abundance versus scarcity mentality in your company. Without your team, after all, there's no business. So ask yourself, "What can I do to show my staff I value them?"**

You can do many things to achieve that—I don't have it totally figured out, either, and am still learning along the way. I will say, however, that I hired both a business coach and someone else with extensive human resources training and job experience to help me with this. Together, the three of us reviewed study after study on companies we most respected and came up with some good ideas. In fact, our game plan is being rolled out at about the same time as this book, so I can spill the beans here!

Incorporate the core values and things you want your company to stand for in your employee benefits. Because my philosophy and value system is based on retiring while you work, we're implementing progressive benefits that align with principles in this book, like travelling or other experiences with loved ones; health and wellness; volunteering and community service; pets; work/life balance and time off; and education. We'll adopt an open vacation policy, where you just make sure the team has your back and you can take off as you need or please to stay sharp and feel balanced; we'll reimburse each employee for health- and wellness-related expenses (gym membership, yoga, home equipment, healthy meal prep, etc.); employees will be reimbursed for plane and hotel expenses to encourage the team to use their time off for experiences and travel; we'll also implement a bring-your-pet-to-work environment (my dog Jolene has the official title of Director of Stress Management, and clients call her the therapy dog); we'll also reimburse for certifications and higher education; and we'll offer employees paid time off for volunteering in areas they're passionate about.

Figure out what values are important to you and your team together, and come up with a plan that gets everyone excited. Not only is it good for your current team, but it's also great for recruiting and your overall culture.

CHAPTER 19

IT'S THE SMALL THINGS

Many times in life, we trivialize the small things and discount their importance. I know how easy it is to get caught up in the day-to-day grind and tell ourselves the (false) story that there isn't time to take a walk and get some fresh air, or do that one hobby you love on a regular basis. This year, I realized I'd been depriving myself of much-needed smaller things that could represent major healing in life, but also help center me and make me a lot more efficient.

For example, after four years of having my office located in a trendy, pedestrian-friendly, progressive neighborhood not a hundred yards from a park, it struck me that I'd been staring out my window every day to see people lying on blankets or in hammocks, reading, writing, or just flat out napping in the grass. And every time, I'd see them, I'd think, *Must be nice—what in the world do these people do to be able to sleep in the grass at noon?*

Well, just last year, I'd introduced a new best friend into my life: a yellow lab puppy Jolene, who I'd trained from day one to come to the office with me and (somewhat) behave. I'd always wanted to have an office dog, and I'd worked my tail off (pun intended) to have my name on the door so I could. All year, I'd struggled to find five minutes between client meetings to take her out so she could use the bathroom, but always in a frenzy. Or I'd ask one of my team members to walk her for me.

My gosh had I missed an amazing opportunity and luxury to take fifteen minutes in the middle of each day, to create space, be present, and walk Jolene across the street to the park. Every day that weather permitted this year, we went out to do our now-ritual, where I throw a tennis ball at least thirty times and she runs her little heart out, smiling so big it's contagious. She's become so good at acrobatically catching the ball, that people notice her, come up to ask about her, want to love on her, or even walk up to introduce their little furry friends to her.

Why is this important? Because those fifteen minutes have become a habit, and my favorite part of the day, almost like a mid-day meditation. I let the stresses of the day pause, and I smile, go out to get some Vitamin D sunshine, be present, and be as happy as a child in a chocolate factory. My dog comes back worn out and behaves better the rest of the afternoon, and I usually have at least one positive interaction with someone new because I've had the opportunity to recharge and get fresh air, which allows me to come back more productive. I cannot stress how much of a difference this has made in my daily routine and mental state.

Early on in the year when I was doing vision board planning with my dear friend, Carly, I'd made it a goal to take up a new hobby that allowed me to play and represented something from my youth. Growing up, I remember my dad would always take me to play tennis—and we had a blast. I haven't played in twenty years, as he isn't able to get around the court like he could back then. And I have the competitive type A personality where if I'm not great at something, I won't do it until I'm perfect at it (which most normal people know isn't realistic or possible).

This year, I took the plunge, signed up at the community center for private lessons and at a clinic to play with others who have equal skill levels. I'm two months in and, once again, cannot stress enough how much I've enjoyed having this youthful time set aside for me to be able to compete and learn something totally unrelated to money and financial planning. Every time I leave, I feel this creative high and energy, which today has prompted me to come home and write another chapter in this book. My mentor George explained that often when we find ways to connect with our youth and play, it liberates the mind and actually helps unlock a creative side that gets stifled when we're busy working our daily jobs.

I share these examples as the small things that have collectively turned into huge things in my retiring-while-I-work journey. They cost little to no money and don't require a huge time commitment, either. Almost anyone can take a walk with a dog or a friend, find an hour to pick up a youthful hobby, and get closer to adopting and achieving the retire-while-you-work mind-set.

CHAPTER 20

THE FOURTH AND FINAL BUCKET

If we don't take care of ourselves, we can't expect to enjoy the experiences and memories we've listed on our vision boards or bucket lists. One night, I was having dinner with my mentor, George, and telling him how I couldn't wait to share my bucket philosophy in this book. He's heard me talk about this philosophy for years, but for some reason, on that particular night, he decided to ask me about the fourth bucket.

I said, "George, come on, man. You know there are only three buckets, and each one has layers, but there are only three."

He paused and said, "Well, that might be true, but it's ironic to me that you never talk about the fourth bucket, which is *you*—and putting resources back into yourself so that you can be strong, centered, and ready to serve." George—1, David—0.

EATING TO LIVE

Oops. I live to eat, period. This is a huge work in progress for me in my own life and personal growth. Now more than ever, we have access to detailed research and information that teaches us how to eat better and, consequently, increase our energy as well as our lifespans. So why don't we all follow this advice?

Consider this Joel Fuhrman quote from his book, *Eat to Live*:[27]

> *The modern food and drug industry has converted a significant portion of the world's people to a new religion—a massive cult of pleasure seekers who consume coffee, cigarettes, soft drinks, candy, chocolate, alcohol, processed foods, fast foods, and concentrated dairy fat (cheese) in a self-indulgent orgy of destructive behavior. When the inevitable results of such bad habits appear—pain, suffering, sickness, and disease—the addicted cult members drag themselves to physicians and demand drugs to alleviate their pain, mask their symptoms, and cure their diseases. These revelers become so drunk on their addictive behavior and the accompanying addictive thinking that they can no longer tell the difference between health and health care.*

A little intense there, Joel. But his book is right on about our struggle to take care of our bodies. It's no secret we live in a society of immediate gratification and we're part of a fast and processed food culture. The pharmaceutical industry *loves* this, as it will sustain their profit margins for decades to come—unless, we flip the switch and start eating to live.

---

27 Joel Fuhrman, *Eat to Live: The Revolutionary Formula for Fast and Sustained Weight Loss*, (Boston, Massachusetts: Little, Brown and Company, 2003).

In the retire-while-you-work framework, taking care of yourself is integral to living a long life so you have the health to take those trips and keep up with active hobbies for years to come.

MOVE.

The human body is designed to move, not sit chained to a desk for eight hours a day and then binge watch four hours of Netflix on the couch (but oh, how fun that can be), just to then lie in bed and scroll through social media the rest of the evening. The average person sits for twelve hours a day, which has become the fourth leading risk factor for global mortality. There are many negative effects to the body when you sit for long periods, ranging from back problems to muscle degeneration to foggy brain.[28]

Let's face it, it's easy to get consumed by work, whether you hate or love your job. But you can work wonders for your body by doing simple things like walking every day, signing up for a yoga class a couple times a week, or finding a hobby that lets you move while also allowing you to have fun and connect with others. I hate doing yoga, but that's why I want to do more of it. I know it's good, and unfortunately, I'm not so great at it. I've yet to find an activity that helps stretch and facilitate the body with total functional strength the way yoga does.

Seeing how sitting through an hour-long yoga class can sometimes feel like six hours at the dentist for me, I've found great happiness recently in taking up tennis again. What's your favorite type of exercise and way to move? Continue doing what you're doing and then find

28 "The Facts: The Human Body is Designed to Move," JustStand.Org, accessed 2018, https://www.juststand.org/the-facts/.

something else that you aren't, and add that to your routine, just once a week even, to achieve a little more balance of movement to the body.

BE STILL AND BREATHE.

As I write this, I've only been able to do five minutes of meditation without checking my watch. That's why I want to learn to meditate.

An innate part of us typically gravitates only toward things we're good at and feel confident and comfortable with. But I've been mentored over and over again to learn that true, meaningful personal growth comes through pain and change, through doing things that our body and mind may resist, but that we know, deep down inside, are probably good for us.

I've always enjoyed working out and playing competitive sports and was never any good at slowing down or "stopping to smell the roses," as they say. I'd show up to a workout class, jump right into it, and then leave during the last ten minutes, the stretching and cool-down period, because I was already moving on to the next part of my day. I had no time for sitting on the floor and stretching, let alone sitting still, focusing on breathing, and training my mind to shut down for ten long minutes.

How ridiculous and short-sighted. I've since been learning how the power of slowing down, resting, or even stopping, is not an unproductive task; in fact, it can become the road to productivity and creativity. Finding one or two times per day to shut your eyes and focus on silence and slow, deep breathing for even ten minutes has been proven to help reset your mind and give you a huge energy boost.

Eating well (or just better), moving more through exercises you enjoy, and finding time to be still through meditation are critical to keeping you healthy in body and mind so that once you get your three buckets set up, you can enjoy the experiences you've been dreaming of.

Remember, the point here is to shatter the old idea of retirement, which is defined by doing all-consuming work for forty years and then starting (or really trying) to enjoy life, often when it's too late to fully experience it the way we'd like. We can do better, enjoy our friends and family, take trips, and do more ... if only we'd learn to retire while we work.

CONCLUSION

Remember, you can retire while you work, but don't make it just about the money or the buckets. I hope that incorporating the ideas and principles I've shared into your journey of retiring while you work will prove to be more valuable than money and all the financial jargon could ever hope to be.

In the process, make sure to take care of *you* so you can be amazing to others. Know who you are, what you stand for, and what your "why" is.

Life is short, and there are many more important things to focus on than worrying or thinking about money. Turn off the news, quit tracking the stock market and logging into your investment account, and, instead, go call your parents and tell them you love them. Or write a note to an employee saying you appreciate them.

Last but not least, I'll leave you with some random nuggets from my crazy brain that have helped me and a few others on our journeys to retiring while we work:

1. Dividends are great.
2. Fear and greed are dangerous.
3. I believe in America.
4. and in you.
5. and in love.
6. Most people are good.
7. Kiss your mom.
8. Make love to your spouse.
9. You can reconnect at any moment—it's a choice.
10. Buy a dog.
11. Buy another.
12. Jump in the pool with your clothes on.
13. Don't burn bridges—you'll be surprised how many times you have to cross the same river.
14. Remember, a person's greatest emotional need is to feel appreciated.
15. Don't major in the minor things—choose your battles wisely; life's too short.
16. Fight for each other.
17. Never say you don't have enough time—you have exactly the same number of hours in a day as Michelangelo, Helen Keller, Thomas Jefferson, Rosa Parks, Mother Teresa, and Martin Luther King, Jr.
18. Learn to say no politely—and quickly.

19. I believe we can conquer our unhealthy views of money.
20. Republicans and democrats need to stop fighting and unite.
21. Take that risk. Start that company. You only live once. You can always go back but you can't redo the opportunity.
22. Fill your buckets.
23. I believe that you can retire while you work.
24. Better yet, I know you can, and think that you'll start on that path now.
25. Retirement is a destination that seems boring, antiquated, and not that exciting of a place. Retiring while you work is a journey that is fluid, exciting, rewarding, and fulfilling.
26. Quit texting so much and call your friends and family.
27. Listen more and talk less.
28. Love harder and judge less—we are all struggling on this journey in our own ways.
29. Change and transition in life are constant—release the fear and embrace it.
30. Mentor back to others the lessons you've learned and pay it forward.

Take the journey with me. I'm just starting—we can do it together.

ABOUT THE AUTHOR

Financial advisor and radio host David Adams is a CERTIFIED FINANCIAL PLANNER™ professional and CPA in Nashville, Tennessee. As president of David Adams Wealth Group, LLC, an independent practice offering securities through Raymond James Financial Services, Inc., David is dedicated to helping his clients live well and retire, too.

For more than fifteen years, David has been committed to the financial well-being of his clients, and now more than ever, he is dedicated to changing an industry he feels is broken. His passion for the business centers around helping people restore vital balance and financial strength through life's many transitions—the sale of a business, loss of a loved one, marriage, divorce, retirement, etc.

In 2016, David launched his Retire While You Work radio show, a weekly show on Nashville Newsradio 1510 WLAC and iHeart Radio, on which he offers financial advice and answers listeners' financial questions. David also launched the companion website, RetireWhileYouWork.com, and e-book to share his philosophy of changing retirement in America and to offer additional resources to his listeners and readers.

Also in 2016, WealthManagement.com and *REPmagazine* recognized David as one of the "Top 40 under 40" independent financial advisors in the United States. Nashville Business Journal honored him as a 40 under 40 in 2017 for his work in the community. He has also appeared on the cover of *Investment News* as "Advisor to the Stars" for the work he does with musicians and songwriters of Nashville.

For 2018-2019 and each of the previous five years, Raymond James Financial Services recognized David as part of the Chairman's Council[29] for the top 1 to 2 percent of advisors in the country. *Music Row* magazine wrote about David helping some of Nashville's finest songwriters manage the financial ups and downs of the music industry. In addition to his professional achievements in 2016, David was recognized in *Nashville Lifestyle* as one of its top twenty-five most beautiful people.

David serves as a frequent resource for many local, regional, and national news outlets such as the *Nashville Business Journal*, *Investment News*, and *Money* as their go-to professional on investment-related matters. He has also been featured in Huffington Post for his retire-while-you-work philosophy.

David is equally committed to the Nashville community. He serves on the boards for Saving Case and Project Alive, the latter of which is a nonprofit that benefits young boys with Hunter Syndrome,

29 Chairman's Council membership is based on prior fiscal year production. Requalification is required annually. Advisors on the Top Next Gen IBD Advisors list are ranked exclusively by assets under management. We solicited nominations from the top thirty-five IBDs by headcount. REP. magazine and WealthManagement.com do not receive any compensation from financial advisors, participating firms and affiliates or the media in exchange for rankings. The ranking may not be representative of any one client's experience, is not an endorsement, and is not indicative of advisors' future performances. No fee is paid in exchange for this award/rating.

a rare genetic disease. He also serves on the board of the Onsite Foundation, which provides scholarships for people who cannot afford therapy for addictions or emotional trauma or who just need guidance to live centered and more balanced lives. He is also a wish grantor with Make-A-Wish of Middle Tennessee.

Visit www.retirewhileyouwork.com to download David's e-book or listen to episodes of the Retire While You Work radio show. To make an appointment with David or for more information about David's office in the Historic 12th South neighborhood, visit www.davidadamswealthgroup.com.

Phone: 615-435-3644 | Fax: 615-435-3931
David.W.Adams@RaymondJames.com
2905 12th Avenue South | Suite 108 | Nashville TN 37204